# The Women's Guide to Lower Scores

ALSO BY KELLIE STENZEL

*The Women's Guide to Golf*

*The Women's Guide to Consistent Golf*

# The Women's Guide to Lower Scores

KELLIE STENZEL

Thomas Dunne Books
St. Martin's Press ❧ New York

THOMAS DUNNE BOOKS.
An imprint of St. Martin's Press.

www.stmartins.com

*Photos by Anthony Loew*
*Illustrations by Precision Graphics*

Library of Congress Cataloging-in-Publication Data

Stenzel, Kellie.
    The women's guide to lower scores / Kellie Stenzel.
        p.    cm.
    ISBN 0-312-32253-4
    EAN 978-0312-32253-3
        1. Golf for women.    I. Title
    GV966.S765 2004
    796.352'082—dc22

                                                2004041791

First Edition: May 2004

10   9   8   7   6   5   4   3   2   1

This book is dedicated to my students. I thank you very much for the privilege of helping you with your golf games. You inspire and energize me and I am so thankful to be able to do what I do. I enjoy my job every day, and while obviously some lessons are easier than others, it certainly is a challenge and great reward when you start to "get it."

I am so proud when you do well and I am here for you when you do not. I thank you for letting me take the terrific journey that is improving and succeeding with you. Golf is so much more than just a game, and that is what makes it so amazing. It is sometimes necessary to dig from deep within and open yourself up, and as a result I thank those of you who have become friends as well as students.

I want to share a few of my students' words to help those of you who might not understand how golf can be so much more than just a game.

*"Golf is a complete escape. There is not time to worry about anything else while you are out here, and sometimes that is a blessing."*

*—Denise*

*"In the beginning the activity was secondary to being with loved ones, but now I enjoy the game itself. This is the first time a sport has entered into my leisure time in a structured manner, and certainly golf has added another layer and made my life fuller."*

*—Gayle*

*"Time is the currency of friendships. We carved out time for friends."*

*—The Palm Beach Par 3 golf group*

"I've learned not to expect total perfection on every swing and to be more accepting of imperfect results. Kellie's expression is "Oh well," meaning to let it go, that it is history. I have found this to be good advice for both golf and life."

—*Irving*

"I learned to play golf in self defense. My entire family, including my husband, had become golf fanatics and I didn't want to be left behind. I needed to be a part of the ad nauseam golf talk at the dinner table and I certainly did not like being ditched all day every weekend. Finally, I fit in with the group. The only problem is—I've become one of them and can't talk about anything else either!"

—*Sloan*

# Contents

# *Acknowledgments*

THANKS

To my family. I love you. To my father for always being there for me and for teaching me the great game of golf. You've taught me such terrific life lessons and to believe in myself and that anything is possible.

And to my brother Rob and his family, Tammy, Shelby, and Kyle.

My ever-faithful O'Malley.

To the membership at Atlantic Golf Club and Rick Hartmann for being so supportive.

Pete Wolverton for your great suggestions, help, and support.

Rich Barber for being so much help with everything and someone I trust.

Tony Lowe for the terrific photos.

Rick and Mary Dytrych and everyone at Palm Beach Par 3 for making me feel so welcome and at home.

Burberry for the beautiful clothing.

# The Women's Guide to Lower Scores

# Introduction: Dramatically and Quickly Lower Your Golf Score

1

**Y**ou can learn to lower your golf score with your present skill level. To this point, you've become basically proficient at each skill area of the game: putting, chipping, bump and running, pitching, sand game, and your full swing, but even on days when you seem to hit more good shots you are often amazed and disappointed when you total your scorecard at the end of the round to see the same old score plus or minus one or two. The goal here is to teach you to better manage your golf game. With simple techniques you can identify your strengths and weaknesses and build a game plan that fits you. Even the best players in the world hit horrible golf shots. They fail to recover from some, but more often they recover and succeed quite nicely by better managing of their misses. By choosing the least-risk/greatest-reward option available, they often make golf look easy. The most skilled professionals and lower-handicapped golfers play their rounds of golf to their strengths.

Some of the methods to help you to lower score will include:

1. Identifying your strengths and weaknesses: Quick, simple tests to help you more clearly see the shots to try more often and the ones to avoid.

2. Simple methods for quick skill improvement: You know what you're supposed to do for each skill, and you could certainly do well on a written or oral exam, but how do you know if you are executing properly? The goal here is to give you very simple suggestions that should immediately cure specific problems as well as give you checkpoints for seeing that your mechanics and execution are correct. These methods will be called shortcut checks, and they will be noted with a checkmark for easy reference. An example of a shortcut check is to hold your finish after you putt to check that your left wrist is still flat.

   You'll also learn quick tips, noted with a small clock to help you to more easily perform specific tasks. The reason for the clock is that these quick tips are designed to save you time and effort. An example is to pigeon toe your feet by turning your toes in when putting to restrict your hips from incorrectly moving. You will find these shortcut checks and quick tips throughout the text, and you may want to focus on the specific areas that you identify as your weaknesses.

3. Specific cures to common problems: Tired of repeatedly making the same mistake? This will include suggestions for correcting errors such as topping, slicing, or missing short putts.

4. Short-game techniques: Very specific questions will be given to help you to identify the best short-game option available to you in each situation. By using a short-game flow chart, better known as your short-game cheat sheet, you'll learn to use the most forgiving shots available to you in different situations. So, in that rare occasion when you do miss a shot, you might actually get away with it. I want you to be able to miss shots your playing partners don't detect—the old "fake it 'till you make it" theory.

5. Better course management: Last, but certainly not least, you'll learn to build your game plan around your strongest skills. After you have identified your strengths and weaknesses with quick tests, you'll learn to build your game to maximize your reward while minimizing your risk. Several example holes are included to help you to learn how to manage your game and to learn some of the thought processes you may use to lower your score and manage your game.

With these techniques and the right attitude you can coach yourself to lower scores and have more success during your round of golf. It is important to remember that golf is a game, and while some take it more seriously than others, it is meant to be fun. From experience, I can honestly tell you it is much easier to have fun when you are playing good golf and having success.

# Skills Test:
# Do You Know Your
# Golf Game?

2

Measure three feet with your putter.

How many of the ten three-footers can you make?

In order to better manage your golf game you have to first be able to quantify your skills. I promise it won't take long, and you don't even have to do it in one session. Try one skill test each time you go to the course. Test, and if you feel you score particularly higher or lower than normal, repeat the test. You may want to readminister the tests throughout the season.

At the end of each test you'll be given your results. These are assigned a color that either will be red, yellow, or green, the colors of a traffic light. A red result is less than desirable and a skill you should avoid using or attempt to improve. A yellow result is average, a skill you should use sparingly and also work to improve. A green result is a positive and a skill you should use throughout your round as well as build into your game plan.

### Can You Make a Three-Foot Putt?

Find a relatively flat three-foot putt (about the length of your putter or slightly longer, assuming it fits you). Place a golf tee in the ground at this distance and see how many putts out of ten you can make.

How many of the ten thirty-footers can you roll within a three foot circle of the cup?

*Results:*
Less than five: red.
Five to seven: yellow.
Eight or more: green.

### Do You Have Distance Control When Putting?

Find a relatively flat thirty-foot putt (ten large steps). Stroke the putt to see how many you can roll within a three-foot circle of the cup.

*Results:*
Less than five: red.
Five to seven: yellow.
Eight or more: green.

### Chipping

Find a generic chip (remember minimum air and maximum roll) where your ball is only several steps from the edge of the green and the distance from the edge of the green to the cup is at least nine or ten steps. Hit ten chips and see how many times you can stroke the ball within three feet of the cup. Remember, three feet is probably just a little longer than your putter.

*Results:*
Less than three: red.
Three to five: yellow.
Six or more: green.

## Pitching—Ten, Twenty, and Thirty Yards

Can you hit a ten-yard pitch shot? A twenty-yard pitch shot? A thirty-yard pitch shot? Remember, a pitch shot is a short-game shot that spends more time in the air compared to the distance in roll. When you pitch, the focus should be where the ball lands, not to where it rolls. Take a towel and place it ten yards (ten big steps) away. Hit ten pitch shots (sand wedge, ball center stance) and see how many times you can land the ball on the towel when it comes out of the air. Only balls that travel in the air count because we are assuming if you are pitching, there is something you have to go up and over.

*Results:*
Less than four: red.
Four to six: yellow.
Seven or more: green.

Repeat at twenty yards.
*Results:*
Less than three: red.
Three to five: yellow.
Six or more: green.

How many of the ten chips can you stroke within a three-foot circle of the cup?

How many ten-, twenty-, and thirty-yard pitch shots out of ten can you land on the towel?

How many of the ten bunker shots can you put onto the green?

Repeat at thirty yards.
*Results:*
Less than two: red.
Three to four: yellow.
Five or more: green.

Notice that at the longer distances a lower percentage of balls landing on the towel is acceptable.

## Sand

Find a greenside practice bunker with nothing particularly difficult like a high lip or a buried lie. Hit ten bunker shots toward the center of the green. How many of the ten are out of the bunker and onto the green?

*Results:*
Less than four red.
Four to six: yellow.
Seven or more: green.

Using your sand wedge, how far does your maximum bunker shot taking sand travel? Do you know your math?

How well do you really know your golf game? After spending a day with Bill Davis, the head golf professional at Jupiter Hills in Jupiter, Florida, I observed him continually questioning his student's ability to know their math. Make an educated guess before you hit your ten bunker shots. Use your sand wedge, and only count the shots where you successfully hit the sand. Do not count any shots that you catch thin and do not take sand. How far do your longest splash shots carry? After you complete the ten shots, pace off the farthest. How far did the ball carry in the air? And was this close to your guess before you hit the balls? *Do* you know your math?

*Results:*
Guessed within three yards: green.
Guessed within five yards: yellow.
Guessed within seven or more yards: red.

You may never have asked yourself this question before, and it certainly is pertinent information. I hope it starts to open your eyes to what you can and cannot do. This knowledge will allow you to make better decisions on the course and avoid attempting shots that have a greater chance to fail than succeed.

## Irons

Pick a shorter iron, a 9 iron for example, and hit ten shots from a good lie. How many of the ten go into the air relatively straight to where you intended to aim?

How many of the ten irons can you hit to your target?

*Results:*
Less than five: red.
Five to seven: yellow.
Eight or more: green.

Repeat this process with a longer iron, a 5 for example. How many of the ten got into the air and relatively straight to your target?

*Results:*
Less than four: red.
Four to six: yellow.
Seven or more: green.

## Fairway Wood

Take your favorite fairway wood and hit ten shots from a good lie. How many travel into the air and go relatively straight to your intended target?

*Results:*
Less than four: red.
Four to six: yellow.
Seven or more: green.

You might want to repeat this test with all of your fairway woods to assess your level of consistency with each.

## Tee Shot

Hit ten tee shots with whatever club you normally use to hit your tee ball on the majority of your longer holes. This does not necessarily mean your driver. If you hit most of your tee shots with a 5 wood, use that particular club for the test. How many of the balls were hit solidly and to your target? An acceptable amount of directional variation would be the approximate width of the fairways where you play the majority of your golf.

How many of the ten tee shots were hit solidly and to your target?

*Results:*
Less than five: red.
Five to seven: yellow.
Eight or more: green.

You might want to test with all of your woods to have a fair measure of your consistency with each. This process could lead you to change the club you use for your tee shots.

## What Club Would You Use for 100 Yards?

Do you know? If you do not, you should consider adding a yardage chart to your golf bag. You will also determine if your distance is a strength or weakness.

Find a target that is 100 yards away. Most ranges will have yardages measured to assist you with this. Hit the club that you can carry in the air this distance ten times. How many times did your ball land within a ten-yard radius of the target?

*Results:*
Less than four: red.
Four to six: yellow.
Seven or more: green.

Were you correct in your club selection to your target? If not, this is another great reason to attach a yardage chart to your golf bag. A yardage chart is a tag listing all of your clubs and the range of distance each travels. It provides a method for you to be able to make decisions for yourself. A yardage chart will be included in the Appendix that you can fill in, laminate, and attach to your golf bag.

What club did you need to carry the ball 100 yards? This can help to determine if distance is a strength or weakness in your game.

*Results:*
Five iron or more: red.
Six iron: yellow.
Seven iron or less: green.

If you fall into the yellow or red category with your ball-striking distance, you can work to improve this. This would also be a good indicator that your short game will need to be a strength.

You can also use this test to check your aim and alignment. Of the ten balls, how many landed within five yards right or left of the flag?

*Results:*
Less than four: red.
Four to six: yellow.
Seven or more: green.

If your results were not as good as you had hoped, was there a pattern to the direction you missed the ball? If the balls felt solid but consistently landed either right or left of the flag, you should check your alignment. If your balls started toward the target, but repetitively curved one way or another, you should check your grip. You will learn later how to check and improve these results.

## Assess Your Strengths and Weaknesses

You can see how practicing to a specific target will tell a lot about your strengths and weaknesses. As a result of taking these short skills tests, you have a better sense of what parts of your golf game are proficient. You might be surprised by some results, having done better or worse with specific skills than expected. The skills that you scored highly on are the ones to use most often during your rounds. Your golf plan can be designed with these skills in mind. For example, if you are not a good long-iron player (a red skill) but you are a good chipper, rather than trying to go over water with your 5 iron, it is probably wiser for you to play to the opening on the right side of the green with your 7 iron and then hit a chip (a green skill).

These tests will also help to identify your weaknesses. The yellow or red skills are the shots to avoid or choose last when you have exhausted all other options available to you. You should focus your attention on these areas for the shortcut checks and quick tips. This will hopefully help you to raise your color level over time and give you more options during your rounds.

You have two choices at this juncture: Be content with your present skill level and design your game plan around your strengths, or learn to improve your skills that are less proficient and increase your options. You do not necessarily have to make an absolute choice here. Being happy with your present skill level and designing a game plan around your strengths, or choosing to improve your skills is something you might constantly ask yourself. You might also find that you drift in between the two over time. When you have more free time for yourself you may want to set aside some practice time to work on your red or yellow skills and to lower your score through a higher shot quality. And when you have less time to work on your golf game and practice you might choose to be content with your skills and to attempt to play smarter to lower your score.

I often find that when I make peace with my present skill level, usually due to a lack of practicing, I play my best. Last winter I made an effort to play golf with two of my students so that I could see what they actually did on the golf course and not just on the practice range. This is not a lesson, but a social round that is often extremely helpful in shaping their lessons and priorities. I feel it is important that as an instructor I need to possess a certain level of skill, or why should you listen to me? So, I do put a little pressure on myself to play respectably when I play with my students.

We were playing at The Bears Club in Jupiter, Florida, and since I had not been playing a lot of golf, my goal to myself was to try to manage the course and to not hit any heroic shots that made me uncomfortable. After seven holes, my student said to me, "You have not hit very many greens, but you are playing quite nicely." I hadn't realized that I had only hit one green in regulation, but I had made six pars and one bogey, which was good for me on this difficult golf course. I then hit the last two greens of the nine in regulation and was very pleased with my round of golf. By making peace with my level of skill that day, I played conservatively and well. You also will want to make decisions based upon what feels best at the moment. As you read through the rest of the book, focus on the sections that your skills-test results identified as your areas to improve.

# The Fundamentals

3

**T**his next section will review the fundamentals of the game of golf. You might focus on this section if you hope to improve your skill levels. I would be misleading you if I told you they were not important. On the contrary, they are the building blocks to your success. Have you ever noticed that you can often tell very good golfers from a distance before they even swing? They look good, very athletic and balanced. This is a direct function of a good setup.

My specific goal here is to give you concrete methods to check if your fundamentals are correct. It is one place where, in my opinion, modern golf instruction can fall short. We often tell you what you should do to get better, but give you little means to check if you are doing it correctly. One of my main goals throughout this book is to give you very specific methods to check that what you are attempting to do is correct. These are known as shortcut checks.

## Grip

There is no compromise for a good grip. The goal is to hold the club in the fingers with your hands in the position that they are when they hang naturally. Your hands are your only connection to the golf club, and gripping it correctly enables:

- **security without tension, allowing you to generate speed**

- **a square face at impact and therefore a straight ball flight**

If you can generate enough speed to create distance and your ball flight is generally straight, your grip is fine! You should never change your grip unless the ball's flight tells you it is necessary. If this is your situation, it will not be necessary for you to read the rest of the grip section.

If your ball flight is straight but not as far as you desire, you can use the following quick tips and shortcut checks to see that you hold the club properly in your fingers.

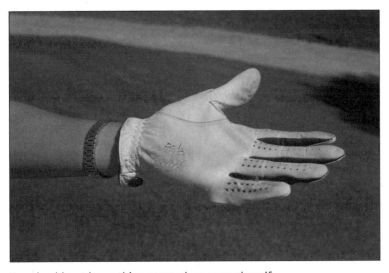

You should not leave this wear mark on your glove if you are holding the golf club correctly in your fingers.

### Holding the Club in the Fingers: Visual Shortcut Check ✔

Check your glove. If there is a hole or a wear mark toward the bottom of your palm, you're probably not holding the club enough in your fingers and therefore it is sliding, causing this mark. This will often require you to hold on tighter, which decreases the speed you'll be able to generate and therefore your distance. This tension will choke away the speed.

### ✔ Holding the Club in the Fingers: Auditory Shortcut Check

Can you hear the swoosh? When you take a practice swing can you hear the club make a swooshing noise caused by the speed? If you can, it is more than likely that you are holding your golf club correctly in your fingers.

### 🕐 In the Fingers: Quick Tip

Learn to balance your club between your index finger and the heel pad of your left hand. If you are holding your club correctly in the fingers of your left hand, you should be able to remove all of your fingers except your index finger from the grip of your club and it should lever securely between your index finger and underneath the heel pad. If this feels strange to you, continue practicing and then simply close your hand around the club for a secure, in-the-fingers grip that will make it easier to generate speed.

To learn to hold your golf club correctly in your fingers, learn to balance the grip in between your index finger and under the heel pad of your hand.

If you are able to hit your golf ball a satisfactory distance but the ball repeatedly curves one way or the other, the cause is often an incorrect grip. Here is a great way to check if your grip is the culprit, and if so, how to correct it.

### ✔ Grip Check: Shortcut Check—Arm Extension

Place your natural grip on the club as you would when playing. Then stand straight up and down. Maintain your same grip, then relax your arms enough to extend them straight out and in front

If your grip is correct, when you extend your arms, the club face should be straight up and down, perpendicular to the ground.

If your grip is "strong," your club face will turn down toward the ground when you extend your arms, tending to produce a hook.

of you so the club shaft lines up with your forearms. After you extend your arms, check the club face. There are three possible results and degrees of each:

One, if the club face is straight up and down so that is perpendicular to the ground, your grip is producing a square face (good), and it is not what is producing your undesired curvature of the ball. Two, if your club face rotates to the left so that it turns down toward the ground, this tells you that your grip is "strong," a golf term that means one or both of your hands is rotated too far to the right. This would tend to produce too much hook (a right-to-left ball flight). If your ball does not hook, do not correct this. But if it does, you have possibly determined a great part of the reason.

I've had the hooks with the best of them. In my most recent case of hooks, every once in a while I would hit a very severe hook and I could not figure out why. I finally realized that I was moving my right hand during my golf swing into a position that was causing the club face to close and produce a nightmare hook. I now can recognize what is causing the hook and correct it relatively quickly by applying a little more pressure in the fingers of my right hand to prevent me from moving it. And while this feels a little odd to me, it never produces that undesirable hook.

You might also check your hands at the finish of your golf swing to see that they are still in the same position they were at the start. Many golfers are unaware that they move their hands during their golf swing. Once you complete the swing, without letting go, bring your hands down in front of you and check to see that they are where they started. If they have moved, you will need to apply more pressure with your fingers to keep them from changing their position during your swing.

Now you need to determine which hand, if not both, needs to be adjusted. Relax your arms again and set the club back down onto the ground in your normal setup position. Look at both hands to note their position at rest. How much of the back of your left hand can you see? Do you see knuckles or fingernails on your right hand? Next, stand up and extend your arms in front of you again. How has the position of your hands changed? The position that your hands moved toward is how they should be at address. This is showing you your natural arm position and the position your arms are seeking during your golf swing. At this point, leave your hands as they are and rotate the grip of your club to the right so that the club face is correctly straight up and down. This is probably requiring you to rotate one or both of your hands more to left.

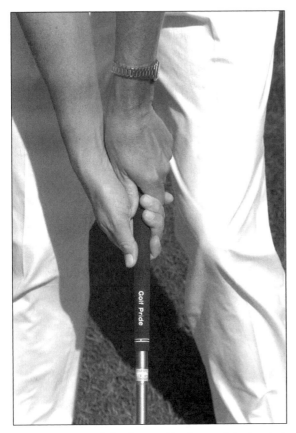

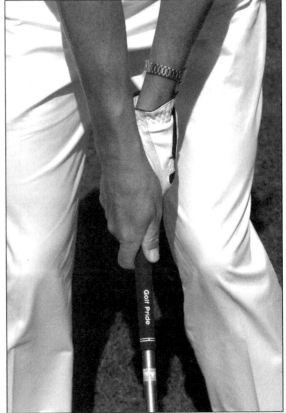

If you see a lot of the fingernails of your right hand at address, this can cause your club face to close.

If you cannot see the logo on your left-hand glove, this will often produce a slice.

✔ The third possible result is if your club face rotates to the right so that it faces more toward the sky, this tells you that your grip is "weak," a golf term that means one or both of your hands is rotated too far to the left. This would tend to produce a slice (left-to-right ball flight). This is very common among women, and the major problem is that a ball that curves to the right, a slice, will travel less distance because a left-to-right ball flight is a speed-reducing spin. The bigger problem, in my opinion, is that the left hand is usually not held enough in the fingers so that you can see the back of the hand as you can when it is hanging. It can often feel uncomfortable to place the left hand in its proper position, and I often see my female students going back to an incorrect left hand because it feels better, even though I recommend otherwise.

If your ball does not slice, do no correcting. But if it does, you just may have discovered the reason. Now you can determine how your hands need to be adjusted to correct this. Relax your arms again and set the club back down onto the ground in your normal setup position. Look at both hands and notice their position. How much of the back of your left hand can you see? If it is positioned correctly, you should probably see most of the logo on the back of your golf glove. You can also draw marks with a permanent marker on the back of your glove to help you to see your proper left hand position. Do you see knuckles or fingernails on your right hand? Next, stand up and extend your arms in front of you again. How has the position of your hands changed? The position that your hands moved toward is how they should be at address. At this point, leave your hands as they are and rotate the grip of your club so the club face is correctly straight up and down. This is probably requiring you to rotate one or both of your hands more to the right.

If your grip is "weak," your club face will rotate up toward the sky when you extend your arms, tending to produce a slice.

## Confirm Any Changes Made with the Golf Ball

If you have changed your grip as a result of the above shortcut checks, you'll want to confirm that the change was positive with an improved ball flight. If the degree to which you rotated your hands either way is correct, the ball's flight should be relatively straight. If you have overdone the change, the ball would curve the opposite way. The golf ball flight is your boss and will tell you when you have made not enough, just right, or too much of an adjustment.

### You Can Learn to Curve the Ball on Purpose with Your Grip

If you understand how your grip controls your club face you can learn to curve your golf ball one way or another on purpose. You do not need to be an advanced golfer to do this, and if you are, you should absolutely be able to curve your ball on demand. I used to take lessons from Gary Ellis, a terrific teaching professional in Hilton Head, South Carolina, and he spent a lot of time teaching me to be able to hit speciality shots. My ability to get out of trouble, smelling like a rose, is a lot of fun and the result of his work.

I also had the privilege to watch Gary Wiren, a PGA golf professional at PGA National, give a free clinic to the members. They came out of the woodwork. It was amazing. There had to be 150 golfers attending the clinic. I had to stay around to watch to see what Dr. Wiren was going to do. He handled them with style, lining them up in groups of five, having them hit one ball at a time. Speaking through a megaphone so that everyone could hear him, he had them change their grip positions to understand how the grip affects the club face and therefore the flight of their golf balls. Taking a group at a time, he first had them turn both of their hands too far to the right. This would cause their hands to seek the position where they hung naturally, rotating to the left and causing the club face to close and produce a hook. He then had them position both of their hands so that they were rotated too far to the left, causing the club face to open and produce a slice. He handled the group beautifully and taught them an immeasurable lesson. I was very impressed.

You should try his method. I know you are thinking that you have enough trouble trying to make solid contact or hit the ball straight, but if you can understand how your hand position affects the club face, you are much more likely to be able to self-correct.

## Posture

There is no compromise for good posture. Posture controls balance, and balance directly affects contact. Posture is especially important for women, because our centers of gravity are our rear ends. That old learning method of trying to sit on a bar stool no longer applies, and if anyone makes this suggestion, do not listen to another word. Another bad piece of advice that you will often hear from "Prince Charming" when you are topping the ball is to bend your knees more. This is also more than likely incorrect. I rarely see women bend their knees too little. The more common problem is too much knee flex, which will incorrectly tuck the rear end under and put too much weight in your heels. If your weight is too much in your heels because you squat rather than correctly bow forward from your hips, your golf swing will tend to pull you off balance, often producing poor contact. This is one of the very specific fundamentals that are especially important for women.

### Posture: Shortcut Check—Shaft on Your Spine

To check for correct posture, place a shaft of a club on your spine from head to tail bone. As you bend forward properly from your hip joint, the shaft of the club should maintain its connection to your entire spine, including your head. If this feels comfortable, your posture is correct in that it is natural for you to bend forward from your hips. If it feels uncomfortable or different than your normal posture, you should use this check to improve your posture and balance.

To check your posture, place the shaft of a club on your spine from your head to your tailbone.

Bend forward from your hips while the shaft maintains its connection to your entire spine, as well as your head.

Many women feel that they are being unladylike when they set up in the proper posture because it can feel as if you are sticking out your rear end. This is how it should feel, and it usually does not look as funny as it feels. You can set yourself up into the proper posture and then look in a mirror to confirm that it really does look fine and athletically balanced.

 **Setup: Shortcut Check—Let Right Arm Hang**
Once you know that you are bent forward properly from your hip joint because your spine is straight, how do you know if you are

the right distance from the golf ball? Take your setup to the golf ball, just as you would if you were ready to swing. Take your right hand off the grip of the club and relax your arm, letting it hang naturally. If when you take your right hand off the club it maintains its position next to the grip of the club, your posture and your distance from the ball are most likely correct. If when you take your right hand off the club and let your arm hang, it moves closer toward your body, you may be standing too far from the ball. Especially pay attention to this if you tend to contact the ball too high, hitting thin or topped shots. If this is the case, step in closer toward the ball until your arm hangs with your hand properly next to the grip.

If after you've checked that your posture is correctly bent forward from your hips and you are still tending to top the golf ball, stepping in closer to the ball cannot hurt at this point and could probably help the situation. When you step in closer it will probably feel a little too close, and this is fine. When you make this correction, it should help you to make better contact sweeping the grass. If you overdo this stepping in you might hit the ground too much (the opposite mistake). You have to let this be OK and adjust the degree to slightly less that you step in on the next shot. The good news is that when you make the opposite mistake you know that you are in the right ballpark with your correction.

When you take your right hand off the club and let your arm hang, if it moves away from your body and outside the ball, you

If your posture and distance from your golf ball are correct, when you release your right hand and allow your arm to hang, it will maintain its position next to the grip of your club.

You may be standing too close if a hanging right arm moves away from your body.

may be standing too close to the ball. You especially need to pay attention to this if you tend to hit the ground too much or contact the ball too much toward the heel of the club. If this is the case, step farther from the ball until your arm hangs properly next to the grip. This also needs to make sense so that you will be able to self-correct. If you continually hit fat shots, where you hit the ground too soon or too much, standing farther from your golf ball cannot hurt.

If you tend to stand too close to the ball it can also adversely affect the path of your golf swing, so standing farther away should also help to improve your swing by naturally shallowing it out with better posture. If you tend to crowd your golf ball by standing too close, you also will have the tendency to contact the hosel (the heel) of the iron, causing a shank. You can recognize a shank by the 45-degree angle at which the ball usually leaves the club face (not fun) and the bad sound it makes. You also can occasionally hear the double hit of the ball contacting the corner of the iron. You can sometimes see a mark in the heel where the ball has contacted the club to confirm this. The shank is also another reason why you will want to stand farther from the golf ball, making it more difficult to contact the heel.

Take your right hand off the club and relax your arm. If it returns to the side of your body, against your rib cage, you are most likely not bent forward from your hips properly but squatting too much. If this is the case, you will want to eliminate some knee flex and feel as if you are pushing your rear end out to straighten your spine. If you bend forward properly and your chest is more over your toes, you can allow your arms to hang properly, with your hands directly underneath your shoulders.

## Ball Position

There is no compromise for proper ball position. It is a fundamental that can affect (positively or negatively) all the rest. For example, if your ball position is too far forward, or more left than ideal, your grip tends to be weak and your shoulders tend to be open (aiming left), affecting posture, aim and alignment.

Your ball position should be centered for your irons, just left of center for your fairway woods, and in line with your left instep for your tee shots with your woods, no matter which one you are using. Adjust your feet for the correct ball position during your setup routine by moving your feet to find the right distance from your golf ball.

### Ball Position: Shortcut Check—Use a Setup Station   ✔

Occasionally double-check your ball positions by using a setup station. Set two clubs perpendicular to each other, with the club just outside the ball facing slightly to the right of your target. Hit several irons (ball centered, heels equidistant from the shaft between your feet); several fairway woods (ball positioned just left of center, left foot slightly closer to the shaft than to the right); and several tee shots (ball farther left in your stance, left heel much closer to the shaft on the ground than to your right).

Notice that when your ball position is moved more forward for your tee shots, the degree to which your left shoulder is higher than your right increases. This will help you to hit more flush from a tee, into the back of the ball, and slightly on the upswing for your woods, maximizing distance. If your setup is not correct for your tee shots, with your shoulders tilted more to the right as

Use a setup station to monitor your ball position. Your short to mid irons should be centered.

Your fairway woods and long irons should have the golf ball positioned just left of center.

Your teed woods should have the golf ball in line with your left instep.

a result of the forward ball position, you will tend to hit pop-ups. To understand what is happening here, the angle at which the club head approaches the golf ball is the angle the ball will reflect off the club. In other words, if the club comes in steeply as a result of your shoulders being steep, the ball will deflect from the club steeply (pop up). If this is the case, you will often see that you are breaking golf tees. Except for the longer tees that are being used for the gigantic new driver heads, it is better not to break your golf tee, but rather sweep the ball off the tee. You can help to feel the proper shoulder tilt to the right by placing a club shaft down your sternum and tilting your body to the right until the shaft of the club touches the inside of your left leg.

## Aim and Alignment

There is no compromise for the ability to aim the face of the club and align your body properly. But, before this can even be possi-

Place a shaft on your sternum and tilt to your right until it contacts the inside of your left leg to feel the proper shoulder tilt for a wood from a tee.

ble or necessary, you must have some type of consistent ball flight pattern. If you miss your golf ball in both directions, it is not only difficult but nearly impossible to know where to aim. For our purposes here, we will assume you hit your golf ball relatively in line with where you aim, and if it is not directly to your target it tends to curve in only one direction. If I do not hit the ball solidly I can only hope it goes to my target.

The two things you need to keep in mind when learning to aim the club face and align your body properly are:

- **aim and alignment must be practiced**

- **learning to aim and align requires visual feedback**

## How to Learn to Aim

Learn how the target "looks" to you when you are set up properly. In order to practice aim and alignment, you will need to use a setup station. Set two clubs parallel to each other so that the ball is between them, and that a parallel line over the ball points right to your target. You'll see that the club to the right of the ball points slightly right of the target and the left club points slightly left. While you hit golf balls between the clubs you should be sure that your feet (heels) remain parallel to the club on the ground. When you do this, the most important thing is to look at your

To learn how it "looks" to aim properly, use a setup station with two parallel clubs. Notice your heels are also parallel.

target throughout your setup routine. This is the visual feedback necessary to learn to aim. When you aim properly, it may look wrong to you at first. This means you are learning how the target "looks" when you are doing it right. When I aim and align properly, the target usually seems too far to the left to me. I've had this feedback over enough time to know that when I feel like I am aiming a little too far left, it is actually correct.

I also get feedback from my golf ball. If I hit a solid shot that feels great but I see it flying to the right of my target, I then realize that I was probably incorrectly aiming in that direction. To double-check this, I will often place a club on the ground across my toe line to confirm my misalignment after the fact. This will help me self-correct later by being more precise with my aiming and picking an intermediate target, rather than thinking my swing is the problem. I also know that when I aim too far to the right, I can start to hit some hooks. By recognizing these signs and reading my ball flight results, I can correct myself sooner before I develop another wrong move to compensate. While two wrongs can make a right in golf, you become less consistent, especially under pressure.

Aim your club face to your target so that the scoring lines of the face are perpendicular to the target line. Aiming the club face has the most direct affect on the direction of the ball. It will deflect wherever the club face aims. Club-face aiming is important on all shots, especially in your short game. I do not think many golfers pay close enough attention to this fundamental. It is

*The Women's Guide to Lower Scores*

a shame to hit a short-game shot that travels exactly the right distance but in the wrong direction.

## Club-Face Alignment: Shortcut Check—Set Face Perpendicular to Aiming Club

You can check your ability to aim your club face in your setup station very quickly and easily. Without changing the direction the club face is aiming, occasionally place your club head on top of the outside shaft of the two clubs in your setup station. If your club face is correct, the scoring lines will be perpendicular to the shaft on the ground. If they are not, correct them relative to the shaft and then replace the corrected face to the ball to see how it sets when correct. You can learn to aim precisely with this feedback. Only change an incorrectly aimed face at address if it matches your ball flight problem. If you placed your club head on the shaft to check where it was aimed and it looked too far to the left, you would only correct this face if your golf ball tends to

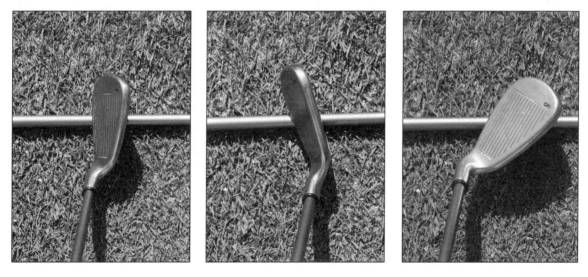

To aim your club face correctly, the scoring lines should be perpendicular to your aiming club.

Club face looking too far left. Correct this if your ball flight is too far left.

Club face looking too far right. Correct this if your ball flight is too far right.

travel too far in that direction. If your ball generally travels too far to the right or travels straight, you need not make this correction. The reverse is true: If you placed your club head on the shaft to check where it was aimed and it looked too far to the right, you would only correct this face if your golf ball tends to travel in that direction. I do not want you to make corrections to make your swing prettier, only more effective, and the only changes are those that will improve your ball flight.

## The Alignment Circle

In order to perform any task, in life or in golf, I believe your concepts can make or break your success. This is the reason for the importance of maintaining proper ball position when aiming and aligning. I often hear my students say, "I do fine when I can aim straight, but I really struggle when I have to change my alignment to aim left or right." From my experience, this most often translates into golfers who simply try to move their feet to change their intended target, rather than walking correctly around the alignment circle, allowing themselves to maintain their proper ball position while changing where the club face aims and their body aligns.

You must "walk around" the ball to maintain proper ball positions and to change your aim and alignment. When you do this, picture a semicircle of golf balls and, while maintaining the position in which the end of the grip of your club points toward your body, rotate around the center ball, changing your intended target with your club face and your body alignments.

When you change your aim and alignment you should not only turn your feet but also "walk around" the ball to change where the face aims, where the body lines aim, and maintain proper ball position. If you were to simply rotate your feet, let's say to the left, without walking around, your ball position relative

Practice walking around the alignment circle to change alignment but maintain proper ball position.

Walk around to your right to aim and align more left.

to your heels would move incorrectly back and most likely make it very difficult to hit a good shot.

You can practice this: Place one ball in the center of a circle of balls. Practice walking around, both to the right and to the left to change aim and alignment while maintaining proper ball position. You should really try this as it makes this concept much easier for you to understand and therefore hopefully retain. I will often take the divot mix off the golf cart and draw this little semicircle around my students' golf balls on the course to help them

Walk around to your left to aim and align more right.

If you simply rotate your feet without walking around the alignment circle, your ball position will be incorrect.

to understand. It is often one of those concepts where I can see the eyes brighten as lightbulbs of understanding get turned on.

This concept is important for all shots, but particularly for tee shots and sand shots. For both, your ball position should be forward or left of your left cheek. If when you aim more left, you do not maintain the proper ball position, the tee shot might "pop up," and in the greenside sand you might incorrectly contact the ball before the sand.

## Setup Routine

There is no compromise for a good setup routine. It will enable you to combine all of your fundamentals (grip, ball position, posture, aim, and alignment) in a specific order that will help you to set up properly, no matter what club you are using. Do you have a setup routine? If you're unsure, you probably do not. I cannot imagine playing golf without one, and yet I see so many golfers who have none. If you do not have a setup routine, you are just guessing that you are set up correctly. To lower your golf score, you will need to do better than just guess.

## Choreograph Your Own Setup Routine

There is no one setup routine that works for all. Just like golf swings have their own individuality, much like a fingerprint, setup routines are specific to the person. They can actually take on their own personality. You've seen them—golfers who have idiosyncrasies that can help you to identify them from a distance. I can often tell who people are by their swings and setups before I can recognize them from their appearances. My college teammate Kristin and I looked very similar in college. Even my own father had a hard time telling us apart from a distance—until we started to set up and swing, that is. Our routines were so distinct that you could easily tell us apart. By choreographing your own specific setup routine, you're committing to repetition and hopefully the benefit of more consistent practice and more consistent results.

Here are two different setup routines that will work. Feel free to make adjustments that help you.

## Club—Hands—Feet

For this setup routine, first set your club to the golf ball, then set your hands to the club, and complete by adjusting your feet. You accomplish this by starting farther away from the ball than you'll eventually be, then setting your club to the golf ball. This is the point where you aim the face to the target. Starting from farther away requires you to bend forward from your hips to set your hands, and this will help you start to allow your arms to hang.

Next, bend forward from your hips and set your hands to the grip of the club. Last, and most importantly, move your feet to

An acceptable setup routine: First look to the target. Set your club to the ball. Set your hands left first. Step your feet to where your arms hang.

where you feel your hands are hanging directly below your shoulders and your feet are parallel to your target line. You may find it takes quite a few steps to find this position; the more relaxed your arms are, the easier it will be to find the point where they hang when you are adjusting your feet.

### Hands—Club—Feet
For this setup routine you will set your grip first, then set your club to the ball and adjust to the proper distance with your feet. You accomplish this by placing your hands onto the grip of a club. It does not matter where you are standing or facing when you do this. Next, standing farther away from the ball than you'll eventually be, step forward with your right foot and bow from your hips to set the club to the ball. This is the point where you aim the face to the target. Start letting your arms relax and hang. The more relaxed your arms, the easier it is to find the point where they hang and enable to you be able to measure your right distance by moving your feet. Last, move your feet to the point where you feel your hands are hanging directly below your shoulders, with your feet parallel to your target line.

### Your Feet Are the Adjusters
Notice that the last step for both setup routines is the same. Your feet are the adjusters. They should be what moves in finding your correct distance from the golf ball. Feel free to experiment with different setup routines. How many times do you look to the target when you set up? Do you like to waggle the club? You might like to take four or five big steps, or would you feel more comfortable with eight or nine smaller steps? Whatever works the best for you is right.

## *Balance*

There is no compromise in good balance. If you're unable to hold a balanced finish position, or if you are falling down during your golf swing, you should not be surprised when you miss the golf ball. You already know that good balance is a function of good posture. So, if you are constantly off balance, you should first check your posture. On the other hand, balance is something that requires experience and must be practiced to perfect.

On more than a rare occasion, I will have a student miss a golf shot because he or she fell off balance, quickly followed by, "What did I do wrong?" My answer is almost always, "Well, you fell off balance." The predictable next question is, "Why did I fall off balance?" Sometimes the answer is an incorrect posture, but more times than not, because I am such a setup stickler, it is that you have to earn good balance, just like you have to earn lower scores.

## Balance: Quick Tip

To quickly practice testing your balance, take practice swings with your feet together. This will help you to make a more efficient motion that will make it easier to maintain balance. You can also practice hitting golf balls from a low tee with your feet together to accomplish the same results. One of my most successful new students, Sloan, will use this tactic to help get back on track if she is having trouble during her golf round, and it almost always helps. This gives her a method to self-correct and the confidence to be able to move past her bad shots more quickly. It is very easy to lose your confidence in golf, and if you have personal methods to get back on track it can help to retain your confidence and produce more enjoyable rounds with lower scores.

For balance, practice hitting golf balls from a low tee with your feet together. Practice holding your finish like you are posing for a picture.

✔ **Balance: Shortcut Check—Hold Your Finish**

Can you hold your finish until your golf ball comes out of the air and lands on the ground? I am continually amazed by how few golfers are able to hold their finish. If they do not finish the same, they should not expect the same results. Practice holding your balance like you're posing for a picture, until your ball lands or even stops rolling. Watch the guys and girls on television. Most of them really hold their finish for a long time. You may not even be aware of how different this can feel. If you have never done it before, try to add this good habit to your practice and your on-course play.

I have a student, Bobsey, who has had terrific success and who is very good at holding her finish. I teach her and her husband, Fred, at the Palm Beach Par 3 golf course in the winter. I can always tell when she is doing well, even if I am not watching her directly, because not only does she hold her finish, but she does a little curtsy at the end that she's not even aware of.

If you have never been to the Palm Beach Par 3, you should go. It is a little jewel of eighteen par 3s on South Palm Beach. The land was donated by the Phipps family to the Town of Palm Beach to remain a golf facility. There are four holes directly on the ocean and three on the intracoastal. It is a very relaxed, friendly atmosphere with a lot of nice people.

# *The Full Swing*

**4**

Full swing.

The success of your full swing is reflective of your ability to set up well. Proper grip, posture, ball position, and aim and alignment will allow your swing to succeed. A repeatable golf swing is not as difficult as we make it, and while the ultimate goal is to lower your score, it sure is fun to hit a good, solid golf shot. There is something to be said about those occasional perfect golf shots that just feel great, sound great, and keep you coming back for more. If you set up well, swing your arms back and through while allowing your body to react, and finish in a balanced position, you should experience success.

## Your Setup Is Your Key to Success

While I might sometimes make my students, especially the new golfers, crazy about their setup and setup routines, I believe the long-term benefits will outweigh the time and effort it takes to learn to set up well.

Your arm swing should pull your shoulders to turn.

## Learn to Swing Your Arms Properly and Let Your Body React

Assuming your setup is respectable:

### Your Arm Swing Should Pull Your Body to Turn

It's a big debate: do you need to think about turning, or should it just happen? While I do not teach everyone the same, I do absolutely believe that if you set up well, swinging your arms and the club back with momentum while keeping your left underarm across your chest, your shoulders will be pulled to turn back, producing coil and power, rather than as a result of a conscious effort. When you turn back you will turn through.

### Coil—Uncoil

When you swing your arms and the club back with momentum, your shoulders will turn back. When you swing your arms and your club forward with momentum toward the target, your body will turn forward to face the target as it uncoils. This is a simple reaction of the body uncoiling as your arms and club swing toward the target.

## The Arms' Swing Generates the Speed, While the Body Supports the Motion

The bulk of the speed you'll be able to generate with your golf swing will come from your hands and arms. I've seen Jim Flick, a very well known and respected golf instructor, hit amazing tee shots while seated in a chair to prove this point. I've been outdriven in a long drive contest by Dudley Hart, a PGA Tour player and the brother of one of my best friends, Kathy, while he was on his knees and I was standing normally.

To generate sufficient speed with my hands and arms, they must be void of extreme tension, aka "the death grip." It is necessary to close your fingers securely around the grip of the club, but not to excessively squeeze the club to keep it securely in position, as long as you are holding the grip properly in your fingers. Unnecessary tension in your hands will tense your wrists and forearms and kill any speed you might hope to generate.

Your arm swing should pull you to turn through.

## *The Body Supports*

Your body and posture will provide balance and stability for your arm swing as you rotate around your spine. If your arms do not work properly due to too much squeezing and tension, the body will often move to try to compensate for your loss in power. This often results in poor balance and therefore poor contact. A sure sign of this is golfers who are off balance and find it very difficult to hold a balanced finish position. I once heard a fellow golf professional say to his student that she should swing the club and not herself. At first this seemed funny to me, but it is also true. If you find it necessary to take a step to catch your balance, this probably applies to you, and you need to practice hitting balls with your feet together while the golf ball is on a tee. This will help to improve your balance and also teach you to generate your speed with your hands and your arms. I am able to hit my golf ball nearly as far with my feet together as I can with them apart.

Rate your finish.

### Rate Your Finish

If you set up the same for each swing, and you finish the same, your odds of contacting the ball the same should be good. If you consistently rate your finish, you can become more aware of finishing the same each time. I am endlessly surprised when my students finish in a completely different, off-balance position, and when I ask them what they think of this position, they are completely unaware. You must be aware of how you should finish to positively reinforce the times when you do it correctly.

Everyone will not finish exactly the same, but here is a rough schedule to rate yourself. Each area it is worth two potential points. Give yourself two points if you successfully complete the task and one if you are close for a partial credit. A perfect score is ten.

All five are shortcut checks to see if you are finishing properly.

A tee in the end of your grip should point toward your target at your finish.

1. Balance: Are you able to hold a balanced finish position until your golf ball lands? Worth two points.

2. Arms relaxed with the club shaft pointed back: Your arms should be relaxed enough to allow the shaft of your golf club to point back away from your target with the shaft of the club resting on your left shoulder. A tee in the end of the grip should point to your target. Worth two points.

3. Right heel off the ground: Your right heel should come off the ground as your right foot rotates up to the toe as your body reacts to your arms swinging forward. Worth two points.

4. Hips facing forward toward the target: Your hips should face forward toward your target as your body reacts to your arms swinging. Worth two points.

5. Right knee close to or touching left knee: Your right knee should be close to or touching your left at your finish position. Worth two points.

## How Fast Can You Swing?

How fast can you swing and not fall down? How fast can you swing and stay in balance? How fast can you swing and still sweep the grass with your club head? Should you swing fast or slow? This is another of those old debates. How many times have you been told to slow down your golf swing, usually when you are failing and close to the point of getting frustrated or mad? We all know that this "Prince Charming" advice is meant to be helpful, but is it? I am very opinionated on this topic, especially when it applies to women. If you want your ball to fly shorter, go ahead and slow down your swing. But keep in mind, if your setup and your golf swing are not very good, it is probably going to be necessary for you to slow down your swing to compensate for these mistakes in order to make contact with your golf ball. You might also need to swing slowly to avoid injury if your setup and/or swing are not technically sound.

But let's assume your setup is good—and by now you know how important this is. Let's also assume that your swing is reasonable. Swinging quickly and continuously will help to maximize your distance. And since most of us are looking to hit the ball farther, swinging your arms and club more quickly will help to increase your club-head speed and distance.

How fast can you swing and not fall down or lose your balance? I'm serious. You should try to find out during your practice time on the range. I really get a kick out of my newer golfers who rear back and take a giant cut at the golf ball, sometimes with success and sometimes not. It is so much easier to teach and learn balance than to learn to swing quickly when you have practiced slowly. What about a long-drive contest among the girls? Try it, maybe the best out of four tee shots. After all, it is possible to be competitive and still friendly. You could play for who buys the drinks at the halfway house. Maybe it would be good to laugh a little more at yourself and just in general when it relates to your golf. There is something to be said about letting your bad shots roll off your shoulders, and laughing at yourself can help. It can be your best option until you have the time to work to improve whatever skills are causing you trouble. Push the envelope occasionally and try these two great ways to practice swinging faster while maintaining balance:

1. **Practice hitting balls from a tee with your feet together. Keeping them together will help you to work on your balance. Learn to swing your arms and club as quickly as possible to hear the loudest swoosh, generating speed and distance.**

2. **With your feet together, practice swinging your golf club back and forth continuously without stopping. Keeping your feet together will allow you to work on your balance while swinging your club and arms back and through as quickly as possible, and it will help to increase swing speed. This can have secondary benefits, as the speed you generate with your arms and club will also produce a more efficient swing.**

## The "L" to "L" Drill

Another great way to learn to generate speed by keeping your grip pressure to a minimum is the "L" to "L" drill. Use a middle iron, a 7 for example, place your hands lower on the grip, and hit balls from a tee. You must keep your hands relaxed enough to allow your wrists to hinge on your backswing and your forward swing. Make a smaller than full swing back and through and allow your wrists to hinge in reaction to the weight of the club head. The shaft of the club should form the letter $L$ between your club and your forearms on the backswing as well as on the forward swing. By being relaxed enough to allow this leverage you will often be surprised by how much speed you will be able to generate with a

The "L" to "L" drill.

less than full swing. This can be a feeling you also transfer into your full swing. If your hands are incorrectly too tight you will find this very difficult to accomplish, so teach yourself to minimize your grip pressure, feel the club head, and generate this necessary lever for speed. If I feel my grip pressure is getting too tight, my goal for improving is to be able to feel my club head throughout my entire golf swing. If you can feel your club head, you are more likely to be relaxed enough to generate speed.

If your wrists or forearms are often sore, tension can be the culprit. If you find it necessary to wear a "bubble band" on your arms, or if you need to put two rolls of tape onto your hands to keep them from getting sore, there is a good chance that you are holding the club too tightly, or not holding it properly in your fingers, which would provide you with the ability to have security without tension.

## Speed Forces Efficiency and Promotes Distance

The good news is that if your golf swing has speed, it is much more likely to be efficient. The continuous swing drill with your feet together often produces some of my students' best swings because the effort to keep the arms and club moving the swing automatically becomes more efficient. It is also an especially good concept for those who tend to make too large of a backswing, which is very common among women because we are generally more flexible than many men. Attempting to keep your club in motion, rather than pausing or stopping the momentum, can help to keep you from collapsing at the top of your backswing. This is why better golfers' swings often look so simple. They look that way because they are efficient and therefore effective.

### The Momentum Drill

To help you to find your proper backswing, try the momentum drill. You will do this without the golf ball. Take your setup with your normal golf posture. With both hands positioned on the club, and bent forward from your hips, point the shaft of the club and your arms directly toward your target. With momentum, swing the club back to the top of your backswing, back through this position with momentum and to a full finish. The momentum of this drill will also help the speed to produce a more efficient swing.

The momentum drill.

### Swing Continuously

If you do not like the word fast, how about continuous? Some golfers cannot relate to the idea of swinging quickly, and I understand. It is very easy to confuse faster with harder. It is important not to add tension when attempting to swing your arms and club with speed.

You may prefer trying to swing continuously, in which your arms and club stay in motion. If you slow or stop your swing, it can be difficult to regain or regenerate this momentum. The only time I might like to see a pause at the top of the golf swing is for those who tend to hook the golf ball. By swinging your golf club continuously, the momentum will produce a more efficient, repeatable swing.

### If You Struggle with Your Full Swing, Practice a Smaller Version

If your ball contact is less than desirable, it is always a good idea to practice a smaller swing. Return to as small a swing as necessary to still make solid contact with the ball. Slowly work your way back to your full swing. I equate this with trying to learn to walk before you try to run. If at any time during my practice I am

struggling, I will either go to a physically shorter club or to my sand wedge to practice the smaller swing of the pitch shot. To help to increase your confidence you should do the same. Limit the time you struggle and go back to a task you can accomplish, then slowly graduate yourself to the original shot. If you are still having trouble, this is when you could use a shortcut check of your fundamentals, determine the cause of your problem, and then apply the appropriate quick tip to help you make the proper correction.

# Stop the Topping: Getting the Golf Ball into the Air

5

To get your golf ball into the air, your golf club should contact the ground with an iron and a fairway wood.

**I**f you are hoping to lower your golf scores, it is helpful to have more solid-contact golf shots. While I might play a very concrete game plan, it is difficult to lower my score if I keep missing shots over and over. Keep in mind that people miss shots all the time, and that this is a big part of the game. But if you continue to top shots, one of the most common problems that I see among female golfers, it is difficult to have much fun and even more difficult to lower your scores. Be it in golf, or life, proper conceptualization can make or break you, and it is the reason for this section. So few golfers understand how the golf ball gets into the air. I believe with better understanding comes a higher rate of success, and fewer worm-burners.

## Understanding What the Golf Ball Tells You

Your golf ball can give you feedback. This understanding is the first step to being able to self-correct. If your golf ball never gets into the air at all, you have contacted it above its equator. This is an imaginary line cut through the center of the ball, just like the one on a globe. If your golf ball travels into the air but not as high as you want, you have contacted the ball below the equator but not swept enough grass. It is necessary for the bottom of your club to hit the ground in order to get the ball into the air the proper amount for each club.

## Divot—Ball and Then Turf!

When a divot is made (sweeping the grass is often sufficient) it should be made after the golf ball. The divot should happen on the target side of the ball. Proper contact for an iron that is being hit from the ground is ball and then turf. I would guess that there are more golfers who do not understand this than those who do.

When I see golfers trying incorrectly to lift the ball by swinging up, most commonly producing a topped shot, I will ask them where the divot should happen—before, under, or after the ball. The most common and incorrect answer is before the ball. But if you think about it, if you hit the ground before the ball you would lose club-head speed before you contacted the ball. This is known as a fat shot. The angle of attack, other than a wood hit from a tee, is descending and the club is on its way down to the ground. For a golf ball to go up, the club head must go down to a minimum below the equator of the ball.

This action is the complete opposite of tennis. Like much of golf, it is counterintuitive. When I play tennis, I have to constantly remind myself to "swing up." Growing up in a golfing family, in which both of my parents were accomplished golfers and my grandfather was a golf professional at Churchville

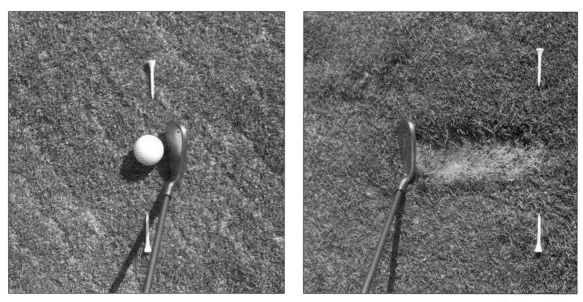

The divot happens after the golf ball for an iron. The ball and then the turf need to be rotated so the tees are up and down and the club is facing the same, as in the photo at right.

Country Club outside of Rochester, New York, the descending motion of golf is my natural instinct. So, you tennis players might have to practice and think "Swing down" in order to get the club down to the ground.

## Terraphobia

It is very common for women to be apprehensive about hitting the ground at all. It could be the fear that it might hurt, or even worse, make a mess. It amazes me how much this fear applies to women and how rarely to men. The reactions of women versus men to the first divot are generally completely different. Women will immediately go get the grass and try to replace it while men rarely even care. And I cannot lie and tell you that it won't hurt if you hit the ground if you hit the ground hard. It can hurt, but it will be necessary at least to sweep the grass. If terraphobia applies to you, pay special attention to your setup and setup routine to make sure that you are the right distance from your golf ball. You can also practice from a golf tee and progressively lower its height as you improve.

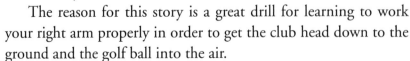 Practice from a low tee with the goal of knocking it out. As you accomplish this goal, slowly lower the height of the tee to the point where it is barely above the ground. Even when the tee is very low, your goal is to clip it out. As you are able to do this, gradually take the tee away and start hitting the ball from a good lie on the ground, pretending that the imaginary tee is still there and that your goal is to knock it out.

## Into the Air

When you make a backswing, your right arm should naturally fold as your elbow points to the ground. Therefore, to get the club head back down to the ground, the right elbow must straighten on the forward swing. This is a lot like throwing a ball. When you throw a ball overhanded, feel how your right elbow folds and then straightens. One of the most amazing examples of this action was shown to me by Mr. Bob Toski, probably the finest combination of an accomplished player and a world-class teacher of all times. I have had the privilege of observing him give golf lessons. I watched him, time after time, place a golf ball into his right hand, fold and straighten his right arm, aim at a golf ball on the ground, release the ball in his hand, and hit the top of the golf ball dead-on. He hit that ball over and over, dead solid center every time. It was amazing! I still try it once in a while and each time I am more amazed at how he could make those golf balls collide every time.

The reason for this story is a great drill for learning to work your right arm properly in order to get the club head down to the ground and the golf ball into the air.

The Toski drill teaches you to straighten your right arm and get the clubhead down to the ground.

## Quick Tip—The Scrape Drill

You can quickly check to see if your club head is low enough to the ground past the golf ball by practicing your forward swing with a scrape drill. If you have any trouble getting the ball into the air, this is a terrific drill. Take your setup. Make absolutely no backswing, only your forward swing. Practice scraping the grass on a semicircle to the left for eight to twelve inches and then go to your full normal finish. Your right heel should come up as your right foot rotates up to the toe in reaction to your body turning forward. This scrape drill works so well because it focuses on the impact zone. If it feels different in how low to the ground the club head stays past the ball, it is a good drill for you. This can be especially helpful for fairway woods.

The scrape drill can help you to get your golf ball into the air.

### Shortcut Check—Hit the Forward Tees

Does your club head stay low enough to the ground past the golf ball to get it into the air? Place two to three tees into the ground in a slight semicircle curving to the left, on the target side of your golf ball. With a practice swing, or with the ball, hit all the tees with your club head. If the ball goes into the air and your club head contacts all the tees, your club head was low enough to the ground to get your golf ball into the air.

### Shortcut Check—Ten Practice Swings

In order to repeatedly get the golf ball into the air from the ground, the club head must sweep the grass. Take ten practice swings. If all ten sweep the grass, your club head is getting low enough to the ground to get the ball into the air. If not, over time, this could be your goal.

## Aim Lower ✔

At some point all of the drills and good intentions might not be enough. Please get tired of topping the ball and aim lower! Hit the ground! Hit the ground! It may seem scary, but just do it. And if it is too much, that is OK. Just let it happen.

## *It Takes Time—You Have to Earn It* ✔

Learning to repeatedly sweep the grass and to get your golf ball into the air takes time and experience. Using these drills and setting the long-term goal of being able to sweep the grass more often should provide you with success and lower scores.

I was playing in an outing in Rochester, New York, at Lakeshore Country Club, in a celebrity pro-am. We had quite a crowd following us because we had one of the local professional football players in our group. The Buffalo Bills football team is a

Hit the forward tees to learn to keep the clubhead low enough to get the ball into the air.

Notice the tees being clipped.

big thing in western New York. I was very happy to have my father there with me to share the day. I dead-topped my first tee shot. While I was a little embarrassed, and would certainly have preferred to have hit a beautiful tee shot, I just smiled, let it go, and played quite well, for me, the rest of the day. I've seen good players hit a lot of bad shots, so do not beat yourself up, stick with your goals over time, and you will hit more successful golf shots and see improvement.

# The Short Game

**6**

**Y**our short game is the quickest way to lower golf scores, and to make up for lower club-head speed. If you do not hit the ball particularly long, your short game can be a great equalizer. While I understand needing to get there by first developing your full swing, you will not be able to lower your scores without a respectable short game. It is very frustrating to arrive on or around the green by hitting beautiful golf shots, only to quickly throw away shots by either choosing the wrong shot-game shot or missing it. I remember four-putting at a college tournament in Memphis, Tennessee, only to be saved two holes later by a torrential rain that cancelled the round.

When I played college golf at Furman University, our team had by far the most success when the majority of our practice time was spent on short game. My college coach, Mic Potter, would say that most bad scores end with a three-putt, and over time I found this to be especially true. In my junior and senior year in college, after we finished a competitive round we spent most of our practice that afternoon on the putting green, focusing on our short game. If we had trouble with our swing we would also hit some golf balls, but it was the short-game focus that helped us to lower our scores.

There are two methods of shaving shots from your score with your short game:

1. **Proper shot selection. You will learn to do this with your short-game cheat sheet.**

2. **Skill improvement. You'll learn to check that your mechanics are correct and be given instructions on how to cure specific problems.**

## Short-Game Cheat Sheet: Extensive and Simplified

While you might have the ability to putt, chip, bump and run, and pitch the ball, do you know when to use which? If you have a better game plan to help you to choose least-risk/highest-reward shots, you can lower your score whether or not you execute the shots to the best of your ability. I want you to hit more effective shots. There is something to be said about missing a shot and still having it run up right next to the pin. Women seem to take each missed shot personally. We tend to think that we are just not very good at that particular shot and take it to heart. What the average female golfer does not realize is that the better players will choose the easiest/least-risk shot that is available to them. Good golfers can make golf seem easy, but a lot of times the reason is they take fewer unnecessary risks. That is what I mean by effective. The shots might not all be pretty, but they work. The job of the short-game cheat sheet is to teach you to choose the right short-game shot for each situation.

## Short-Game Concepts and Definitions

If you are going to lower your scores, you must take responsibility for understanding these basic concepts. By learning and understanding them you should immediately see improvement. I hope that they make sense to you, as that will make them easier to remember and retain.

### Short-Game Definition

How far do you hit your sand wedge? You are considered to be in your short game when there is less distance between you and your target than a full swing with your sand wedge. As you can see by this definition, each of us might start short game from a different distance. It is a very important part of knowing your own golf game. By being specific you can pinpoint when to start to use your short-game cheat sheet and when you will need your yardage chart. If you are farther from your target than a full swing with your sand wedge, you should use your yardage chart. This can range from as short as thirty yards to a high end of sixty yards for most women.

Now, you and I are not Tiger Woods or Michelle Wie, a new young phenomenal golfer who if you have not heard of her yet, you will. I read in an article that she hit a short-game shot of eighty yards, which seemed amazing to me. This is another reason to play your own golf game and not that of others.

### Chipping Definition

A chip is a short-game stroke consisting of minimum air and maximum roll. A chip will be hit from within five steps from the edge of the green. The ball will land on the putting surface when it initially comes out of the air and roll a greater distance that it carried. You can land the ball one to two steps onto the putting surface and choose the proper club, based upon the percentage of roll needed.

Chip when you are within five steps of the edge of the green and need more roll than carry.

Bump and run when you are six or more steps from the edge of the green and need more roll than carry.

### Bump-and-Run Definition

A bump and run is a short-game stroke in which the setup and the motion are just like that of a chip. A bump and run will be hit from six steps or more from the edge of the green, through short, manicured grass, where the ball will initially land short of the green with a lower trajectory and then run up. This is a short-game shot commonly used in Europe, especially on the links of Ireland, England, and Scotland, to keep the golf ball from being affected by the prevailing winds.

### Pitching Definition

A pitch is a short-game swing that will produce a higher ball flight so that a greater percentage of its distance is carried in the air compared to its amount of roll. A pitch will generally be hit using your sand wedge, with the ball positioned in the center of your stance. A pitch shot is a high, lofty short-game shot that is very pretty but more risky. I find it common that golfers have a hard time remembering the difference between a pitch and a chip by definition. A lot of terms are confusing and do not necessarily make sense, but one way you might remember what a pitch shot should look like is this example one of my students, Amanda, and I came up with. If you take the letters in pitch (P,I,T,C,H) and attach the following words, it might help you to remember.

P=play

I=in

T=the

C=center

H=high

Play In The Center
(the ball position) and
the ball should travel High.

Pitch when you need more carry than roll.

## Short, Manicured Grass

Short, manicured grass should not be considered ground to carry when comparing ground to carry versus room for roll to determine the best shot option available to you. This is an especially important distinction because many of you are selecting more difficult short-game options because you do not realize that your ball will absolutely roll through short, manicured grass.

As you position your golf ball more in line with your right foot, you receive less loft and more roll.

## The Smaller the Swing or Stroke the Less the Chance for Error

An error with a small swing translates into a small error. An error with a larger swing translates into a greater error. The smaller swing will generate less speed and therefore less error. An example is a car accident. One that happens twenty miles per hour will do much less damage than one at fifty-five miles per hour. So, the moral of this story is that you want to be able to use the smallest stroke or swing whenever possible.

Differing ball positions within your stance produce different effective lofts—aka higher and lower shots. As you vary your ball position within the width of your stance, the effective loft of your club face changes. As the loft changes, due to varying ball position, so does the trajectory of the ball.

## Left for Loft—Right for Roll

Change your ball position more toward your right foot, while maintaining the end of your club to your belly button. Notice that the club face will lose some of its loft, which will produce a lower shot with more roll. It is especially important you understand that when you have a bad lie and need to move your ball position back to insure contacting the ball before the grass, because you will receive more roll you will need to adjust the necessary swing size accordingly.

 If you understand this concept you can also adjust your setup for being lazy if you do not have the right club and do not feel like walking all the way back to your golf cart. While I am not giving you the OK to be lazy and do this, I am realistic. If you have your sand wedge and you want to chip, but a 9 iron might be more appropriate for the amount of roll needed, you can take your sand wedge and position the ball back in your stance, in line with your middle toe, and lean your weight excessively left. Both of these adjustments will serve to lessen the loft of the club and your sand wedge will react more like a 9 iron, producing more roll. You are effectively turning your sand wedge into a 9 iron with your setup.

A ball centered in your stance will produce a shot matching the loft the manufacturer has set as standard. Keep in mind that standard can be different for different manufacturers. Another variable that can make golf more confusing is that the loft set for each club can be different among manufacturers. A sand-wedge loft can vary anywhere from approximately fifty-seven degrees down to fifty-four degrees, and each sand wedge will still say *S* on the bottom. If you feel you hit your sand wedge too high and short or too low and far, you might want to have the loft checked. A machine can measure loft to be sure that there is the proper amount of difference between each club.

A centered ball position produces the actual loft of the club.

As you position your golf ball more forward in your stance, or more toward your left foot, while maintaining the end of the grip to your belly button, you'll see a more lofted club face, producing a higher shot with less roll. Always be wary of doing this because you need a near perfect lie to attempt this shot. Also, a large swing is required due to the increased loft, producing a higher risk level. I rarely if ever will try this and if I do position my golf

As you position your golf ball more in line with your left foot, you receive more loft and therefore less roll.

ball more left in my stance to hit a higher and softer pitch shot, I only move the ball very slightly forward.

### Assess the Lie

The better the lie of the ball, the more options you have to choose from. The worse the lie, the fewer the options. In other words, if my golf ball is perfectly perched on top of short, manicured grass, I can choose from all three of the short-game choices: putting, chipping (bump and run), or pitching.

If the ball is nestled down in long, wiry grass, I will have fewer options. A bad lie would most likely eliminate my ability to putt or pitch, and I would have to chip or bump and run the golf ball. The reason is that if the ball is sitting in a way that makes it difficult for me to get the bottom of the club cleanly to the bottom of the ball, I need to position the ball farther back in my stance and have my weight favor my left foot. Due to lie, this is more of a chipping setup, producing a lower ball flight that will result in more roll. Because the first priority is to get the ball out of the long grass, I will have to sacrifice some of the ability to hit a high, soft shot.

### The Length of the Grass Where the Ball Lands Will Affect the Amount of Roll

The longer the grass where the ball lands, the less the ball will roll. The shorter the grass, the more the ball will roll. In other words, different grass lengths will produce different amounts of roll.

### The Trajectory of the Shot Will Affect the Amount of Roll

The higher the trajectory of a golf shot, the less it will roll when it lands. The lower the trajectory, the more it will roll.

## Order of Priority: Putt, Chip (Bump and Run), Pitch

1. Putt whenever you can.

2. Chip (bump and run) when you cannot putt.

3. Pitch when you have eliminated all other options.

Probably one of the most important messages for lowering your score is to remember this order of priority for your short game. It is the premise around which the short-game cheat sheet revolves. By using this order of priority for your short-game shot selection you will enable yourself to lower your scores simply by choosing the least risk with the greatest reward. This pattern alone should provide you with a tool to lower your score. While the short-game cheat sheet will help you be more specific in selecting the best shot for each situation, it will also help you to choose the proper club.

There are two versions of cheat sheets. The first is more extensive and includes everything you need to know to make the best decision for all of your short-game possibilities. The second is a more simplified version of the first that should be easier to apply to your on-course play, and you might wish to attach a copy to your golf bag along with your yardage chart and uneven-lie cheat sheet. A copy of the simplified short-game cheat sheet is included on page 222 in the Appendix.

# Short-Game Cheat Sheet

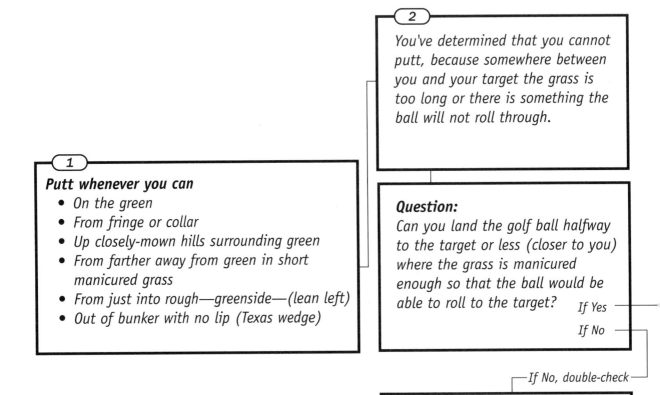

**2**

You've determined that you cannot putt, because somewhere between you and your target the grass is too long or there is something the ball will not roll through.

**1**

**Putt whenever you can**
- On the green
- From fringe or collar
- Up closely-mown hills surrounding green
- From farther away from green in short manicured grass
- From just into rough—greenside—(lean left)
- Out of bunker with no lip (Texas wedge)

**Question:**
Can you land the golf ball halfway to the target or less (closer to you) where the grass is manicured enough so that the ball would be able to roll to the target?   *If Yes* ——

*If No* ——

——*If No, double-check*——

Do you have a greater distance in ground to carry (long grass or sand, for example), compared to the distance of short manicured grass where the ball will roll?
*If Yes* ——

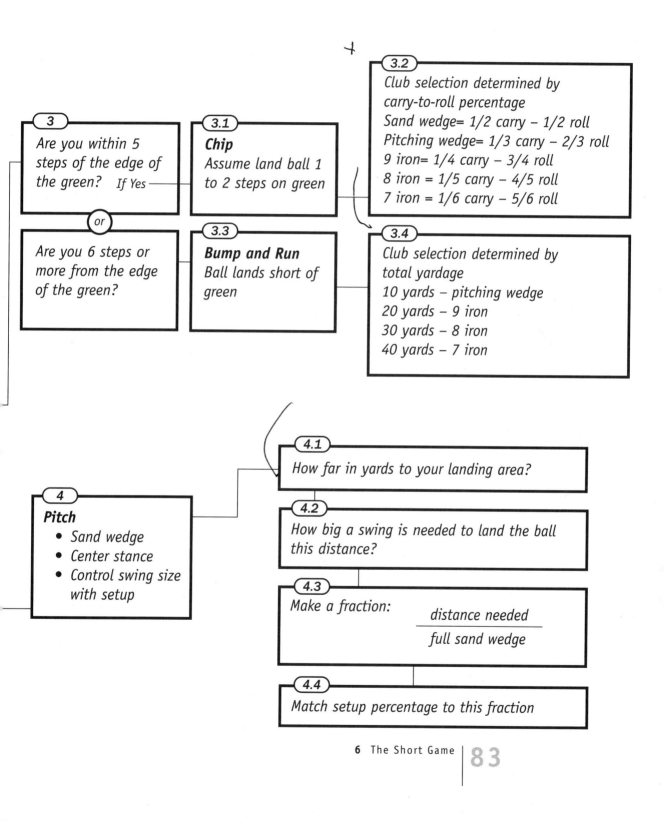

**3** Are you within 5 steps of the edge of the green? *If Yes*

*or*

Are you 6 steps or more from the edge of the green?

**3.1 Chip** Assume land ball 1 to 2 steps on green

**3.2** Club selection determined by carry-to-roll percentage
Sand wedge= 1/2 carry – 1/2 roll
Pitching wedge= 1/3 carry – 2/3 roll
9 iron= 1/4 carry – 3/4 roll
8 iron = 1/5 carry – 4/5 roll
7 iron = 1/6 carry – 5/6 roll

**3.3 Bump and Run** Ball lands short of green

**3.4** Club selection determined by total yardage
10 yards – pitching wedge
20 yards – 9 iron
30 yards – 8 iron
40 yards – 7 iron

**4 Pitch**
- Sand wedge
- Center stance
- Control swing size with setup

**4.1** How far in yards to your landing area?

**4.2** How big a swing is needed to land the ball this distance?

**4.3** Make a fraction:  $\dfrac{\text{distance needed}}{\text{full sand wedge}}$

**4.4** Match setup percentage to this fraction

## *How to Use the Short-Game Cheat Sheet*

The short-game cheat sheet assumes that you are in your short game. First, you need to confirm that you are in your short game. You first determine this by knowing when you are closer to your target than the distance you achieve with a full swing with your sand wedge. As you can imagine, this distance can be different as it is based upon the individual. Once you have determined that you are within this distance, you can start to utilize your short-game cheat sheet.

The short-game cheat sheet assumes you have a good enough lie so that all short-game options are available to you. If your golf ball is not in a good lie, you will have to utilize more of a defensive chipping-type setup to get the ball out of trouble.

### Assess the Lie of Your Golf Ball

The first step in selecting the proper shot for the situation is to assess the lie of your golf ball. If the lie is good, where the ball is sitting on top of the grass, you'll have the option of all the shots

available to you. If the ball is resting down deeply in the grass or another obstruction, you'll need to proceed to a more defensive, rescue-and-recovery setup like that for a chip. By positioning your golf ball more in line with your right foot and placing a greater percentage of weight on your left foot (the worse the lie, the more you should exaggerate this position) you will make steeper the angle of attack of the club head into the ball. As you place more weight on your left foot, feel how your left shoulder gets lower. This shoulder angle is what produces the more descending blow. This steeper angle will allow the club to contact the ball before all the thick grass, and because the club face will have less loft as a result, you should plan for more roll. The steeper angle will help to extract the ball up and out of the tough lie.

## Mental Tip

You need to be sure to hit the ground and get the club down into the grass. While this might seem counterintuitive, it is getting the bottom of the club down to the bottom of the ball and into the

A bad lie requires a more defensive chipping setup with the ball in line with your right foot and your weight on your left.

grass that allows it to pop up and out of the longer grass. If this is your case, keep aiming lower until you "find the ground."

Once you have determined that you are in your short game and that you have a good lie, start with box #1 and putt whenever you can.

Putt whenever you can:

Assuming your lie is good, putt whenever you can. Because the golf ball does not travel into the air when you putt, and because there are fewer moving body parts, putting will always be your least risky shot. It allows you to maximize your reward with the least amount of risk.

### Situations Where You Should Consider Putting

Putt from the fringe.

1. On the green—obvious!

2. From the fringe or collar surrounding the green. Your putter is not simply for on the putting surface. You should almost always putt from the ring of slightly longer grass surrounding the green that might slow your golf ball down, but usually the necessary adjustment for this is very small.

3. From closely mown hills surrounding the green. Even though the hill surrounding the green can be quite steep, if the grass is closely mown the ball will successfully roll up the hill. This is especially true of the newer golf courses. The steeper the hill, the larger the stroke you will need to take to compensate.

4. From farther away from the green with short manicured grass. The approach to the green is often very closely mown. This allows you to be able to putt from quite a distance back from the green, even up

Putt up closely mown hills surrounding the green.

to fifteen yards, depending upon the length of the grass. You will need to assess the length of the grass to decide how large of a putting stroke is necessary. The longer the grass the more you will need to increase the size and therefore the speed of your putting stroke.

5. From just off the putting green in longer grass. If your golf ball rolls off the green and settles into the longer grass around the green perimeter, you can often use your putter. Even though the golf ball may be setting down in the long grass, a slight lean to your left in your setup will help to increase the steepness of the putter head into the ball and "pop" the ball up and out so that it will roll. Be sure to get the putter head down and into the grass. This is a short-game shot that most golfers do not realize is available. Because the ball becomes slightly airborne when it is originally contacted, due to the leaning

Putt from farther away from the green on short, manicured grass.

Putt from just off of the green in longer grass. Lean your weight to your left.

left, the longer grass that looks to be so much in the way will not affect the golf ball whatsoever.

6. From a greenside bunker with no lip. Also known as a Texas wedge, if the bunker next to your green has no lip, you can and should putt the ball. This is less risky than taking a blast shot with your sand wedge. The courses where I grew up playing, Seneca Lake Country Club and Wayne Hills Country Club in western New York, both had this type of flat bunker around the edges of the green where you could putt, but many of the newer, more difficult courses do not have as many of these.

Try each of these putting techniques in practice before you use them on the golf course. Aside from the obvious putting from the green or the fringe, the other possible situations in which you could and probably should use your putter need to be practiced before you use them in your rounds. When you attempt a new shot, it might take a little trial and error before you have the proper feel for success. We have a lot of closely mown hills surrounding the greens at Atlantic Golf Club, where I am privileged to teach in the summer, and I have practiced putting from these areas enough to know that I need a little larger stroke than I think.

After you have exhausted all of your possible putting options and have determined that you cannot putt, advance to box #2 and ask yourself the questions in the boxes below to determine your next-best option. Can you land the golf ball halfway to the target or less (closer to you) where the grass is manicured enough that the ball would be able to roll to the target? In other words, do you have more room for potential rolling than the area that you need to carry? If the answer is yes, there is more room for the ball to roll, where you can land the ball closer than halfway between you and the target, you should advance to box #3 and decide whether you need to chip or bump and run.

You've determined that you absolutely cannot putt because there is something between you and your target that the golf ball will not roll through, like longer grass or a bunker. You've also determined that there is more room for roll when compared to the necessary amount of carry. Now the decision-making begins. Ask yourself the questions below box #3. Do you chip? Do you bump and run?

## More Room for Roll—Chip or Bump and Run

If you have more room for roll than ground to carry, and I hope that you do, because it is your next best option relative to putting, you should either chip or bump and run the ball. Remember when making this decision that short, manicured fairway grass is not considered ground to carry. A chip and a bump and run will have smaller percentage of its total distance in carry when compared to the roll.

When deciding whether to chip or bump and run, ask yourself the questions below box #3. Are you within five steps of the edge of the green, or are you six steps or more from the edge of the green? If you are within five steps of the edge of the green, you should advance to box #3.1 and chip your golf ball.

## More Room for Roll—Within Five Steps of the Edge of the Green—Chip

If you have more room for roll than ground to carry and you are within five steps of the green, you should chip. When you are chipping you will land the ball one to two steps onto the putting surface. You should land the ball one to two steps onto the green that is relatively close to you and then the ball will roll to the pin. The advantage is you'll only need a small stroke. This has much less chance for error as it is easier to hit a target that is close to you than one that is farther away.

Once you've determined that you should chip your golf ball because you are within five steps of the edge of the green and have room for roll, you should advance to box #3.2 to determine your club selection.

## Club Selection

Choose your club for chipping based upon the percentage of roll you need. You can be very specific and attempt to remember the percentage of carry to roll for your sand wedge through your 7 iron, or you may choose to keep it simple. If you choose to keep it simple and need a little more roll than carry, use your pitching wedge. If you need a lot more roll than carry, use your 7 or 8 iron. If you choose to be more exact with your club selection, compare the distance from your ball to one step on the green with the total distance of the chip. An example of this would be if you were four steps to the edge of the green and the total chip was twelve steps, four compared to twelve is one-third. Use the club that gives you one-third carry and two-thirds roll, which would be your pitching wedge. We are assuming medium speed, relatively flat greens here. If the green is undulated or unusually uphill or downhill you might need to adjust your club selection.

For uphill, take less loft. For example, use a 7 instead of an 8 iron. Since you will be going against gravity uphill, you will receive a lower percentage of roll than on a flat surface. Rather than needing to take a larger stroke, you can simply change to a lesser lofted club to make up for the loss of roll because of the uphill.

For downhill, take more loft. For example, use a sand instead of a pitching wedge. Since you are going with gravity on the downhill, you will receive a higher percentage of roll than on a flat surface. Rather than taking the chance of the ball getting too far away from you, you can simply change to a more lofted club and adjust for the increase in roll because of the downhill.

## Percentages of Carry to Roll when Chipping

If you can only remember one, remember that the pitching wedge is one-third carry and two-thirds roll. These percentages only apply for chipping when your golf ball initially lands onto the putting surface when it comes out of the air. We are assuming medium speed, relatively flat greens.

**Sand wedge = ½ carry and ½ roll**

**Pitching wedge = ⅓ carry and ⅔ roll**

**9 iron = ¼ carry and ¾ roll**

**8 iron = ⅕ carry and ⅘ roll**

**7 iron = ⅙ carry and ⅚ roll**

**6 iron = ⅐ carry and ⁶⁄₇ roll**

Having asked yourself the questions below box #3 and determined that you needed more roll and were six steps or more from the edge of the green, advance to box #3.3 and bump and run.

## More Room for Roll

Six or more steps from the edge of the green bump and run. If you've determine that you have more room for roll, and you are six or more steps from the edge of the green, you should bump and run. While a bump and run and a chip both have less time in the air and more time rolling, their setups are the same and their strokes are similar. You may find that the stroke size needed for a bump and run needs to be larger than that for a chip. The major difference between a bump and run and a chip is that a bump-and-run ball will land short of the putting surface when it originally comes out of the air and then run up, while the chip will land onto the putting surface when it originally comes out of the air. The reason for this differentiation is the cut of the grass, which is generally longer in front of the green, and therefore the percentages of flight to roll mentioned earlier in chipping will not apply to bump and run. Consequently, you will determine your club selection based upon the total distance necessary for the shot.

Once you've determined that you should bump and run because you have more room for roll and are six steps or more from the edge of the green, you should advance to box #3.4 to determine your club selection.

Club selection for bump and run:

This selection is based upon the total distance of the shot needed.

**10 yards = pitching wedge**

**20 yards = 9 iron**

**30 yards = 8 iron**

**40 yards = 7 iron**

**50 yards = 6 iron**

The shorter the total distance for your bump and run, the more lofted the club you will need, and the greater the total distance of your bump and run, the less lofted the club. This will allow you to take a smaller swing from a greater distance. Once again, the smaller the swing the less the chance for error. I like to experiment with my students in choosing the best clubs for them. One of my students, Denise, was having trouble with her bump and runs, so we spent a percentage of her lesson time on just this shot. Her concepts and fundamentals greatly improved over this two-week period, and we also were able to confirm that her club of preference for her bump and runs was a 9 iron, except for the very short bump and runs where she would use her pitching wedge.

As with Denise, it is usually very obvious what club works best for each person. Most often it is the lesser lofted club that allows the golfer to be able to take a smaller stroke, with less chance of error as a result. With the bump and run, much like that for the chip, if you make a mistake and do not quite sweep the grass you'll often get away with it and the ball will still roll onto the putting green.

Feel free to adjust the club you use for different distances if you find more success with your own club selection. These are merely suggested yardages for each club. This entire short-game cheat sheet is merely a framework from which you can make adjustments that work better for you. You should always play to your strengths and if you have a favorite short, you should always use it whenever possible. Note: you may need to consider a more lofted club than suggested for the longer bump and runs if there is a more significant amount of ground to carry. If this is the case, you will require a larger swing.

If when you asked yourself the questions below box #2, you determined that you could not land the ball less than halfway, closer to you and having more room for roll, you should double-check with a second question: Do you have a greater distance in ground to carry (long grass or sand, for example) compared to the distance of short manicured grass where the ball could roll? If the answer is yes, that you do have more ground to carry than room for roll, you will advance to box #4 because you have determined that it is necessary for you to pitch the golf ball.

## More Ground to Carry Than Room for Roll—
## You Have to Pitch

You've ruled out putting. You've ruled out chipping and bump-and-running because there is something between you and your target (long grass, bunker, or water) that requires more necessary air time than room for roll. Once you've ruled out all other options, you'll have to pitch.

Pitching is your last option because a greater percentage of the shot needing to be carry, this will often require a larger swing. The larger swing has greater risk. Also, if you are pitching there is something you need to go up and over. If by chance, you make a mistake and you do not hit the ground with your club. The ball will not get into the air, and the ball probably will be smack dab in the middle of what ever you needed to get over.

Once you've determined you must pitch the ball, you'll:

- **use your sand wedge**

- **position your golf ball in the center of your stance**

- **point the grip end of your club to your belly button**

## How Big a Swing Is Necessary?

Once you've decided it is necessary to pitch, you will then need to determine how large of a swing is necessary to carry the ball to your desired landing area. The first step to your distance control pitching is to advance to box #4.1 and determine how far it is in yards to your landing area. As you advance to box #4.2, asking yourself how big of a swing is needed to land the ball this distance, you will determine this in box #4.3 by comparing the distance to your landing area to the distance of your full sand wedge.

$$\frac{\text{distance to the landing area}}{\text{full sand wedge distance}}$$

An example: If you are thirty yards to your landing area and a full swing with your sand wedge is forty yards, thirty is three-quarters of forty. Therefore, you'll need a three-quarter swing.

## Are You Able to Judge Distances?

This system of using a fraction to determine your necessary swing size is all well and good, but we are assuming that you can judge ten, twenty, and thirty yards. We practiced in college the ability to measure ten yards so we could have a very good idea that one of our strides was exactly one yard. If you have a good idea visually of ten yards, you can determine how many increments of ten yards is between you and your target, helping you to have a good idea of the estimated distance.

If you do not have a good feel for judging distance in yards, you can start to learn by making an educated guess before your shot. Go ahead and hit your shot, and then afterwards you can pace with one large step equaling approximately one yard, from where you hit the ball to your target to get a feel for the true distance. Even if you know the distance in hindsight, you can learn to be able to judge distances better over time with this method of pacing. Once you have come up with this fraction in box #4.3 advance to box #4.4 and match a setup percentage to the fraction.

## Control Your Swing Size with Your Setup

To assist in controlling your distance, use your setup to help determine your swing size. The smaller the distance needed, the smaller the setup you will take. By gripping lower on the handle and narrowing your stance, the shorter lever and the increased resistance provided by keeping your feet together will only allow for a smaller swing, and therefore the ball will travel a shorter distance. As you require greater distances, place your hands higher and your feet wider proportionally. Providing you with a longer lever and more flexibility allows for a larger swing and therefore greater distance.

## Distance Control Takes Time

Learning to control the distance you pitch the ball in the air with your sand wedge takes time, practice, and feel. This is something I do not think you can practice too much. The feel it takes to be able to control your distance takes experience and repetition with feedback; in other words, you have to practice. I suggest finding ways to make it fun. You can practice hitting to specific targets and not stop until you accomplish your goal. It can also be fun to have a contest with a friend to play match play, seeing who can land the ball closer to the chosen target. If you are playing a match where each shot is one point, you could vary your targets to teach yourself to be able to adjust your distance upon command, just as you would have to do during a round of golf on the course.

This explanation for using the short-game cheat sheet is to help you to learn to use it yourself. Over time, these questions will seem obvious and unnecessary, but I think that very often it is assumed that the average golfer knows what they do not. Take this with you and practice running through the chart. Once you are comfortable with the extended version and know how to use it to choose the right shot, you probably will then find it only necessary to use the simplified version.

## *Short-Game Skill Improvement: Shortcut Checks and Quick Tips*

Now that you're able to select the least risk/greatest reward short-game shot by using your short-game cheat sheet, you can focus on improving the skills that you scored the lowest on in the skills test area. This area will include ways to check if your technique is correct (shortcut checks) and quick tips to help you to improve. Your shortcut checks will be marked with a check and the quick tips with a clock for all of the time you will save by doing them. Drills and quick tips are meant to save time, not to be a punishment. I had a student who used to call his drills "the penalty box." While this was not my first choice for what they were called, he would do them as needed and make the necessary change because the quick tip enabled him to feel the proper motion with the immediate kinesthetic feedback of correction.

While there are a multitude of topics related to each area of the short game, the focus here is to cut to the chase and concentrate on the more important ones for each area.

## Putting

The two skills you must possess to be a good putter are to be able to aim your putter face correctly at your target, especially important on short putts, and to be able to control your distance, especially important on long putts. I think these skills are often taken for granted. We run a ladies' short-game school each spring at Atlantic Golf Club. This year we checked their putter face alignment with a laser that we place on their putter after they attempted to aim their face on a short putt. While some of them were very good, there were others who were significantly off with the face alignment, even on a four-foot putt. Putter-face alignment is something that better players are constantly practicing and adjusting. If you do not aim your putter face properly as a general rule, you will need to compensate for this mistake by altering the path of your stroke. An example: if you tend to aim your putter face too far to the right you have to compensate by altering the path of your stroke to the left in an effort to pull the ball back to the target. Now, this can work. It's true that two wrongs can make a right in golf, which is why you will see so many different swings that work, but under pressure the more compensations that you have to make the less likely they are to hold up.

Proper setup and posture will make both of these skills more attainable. Bend forward from your hip joint and allow your hands to hang directly below your shoulders. You should feel as if your chest is over your toes. This may also make you feel as if you are sticking out your rear end, and this is fine, ladies.

## ✔ Putting Posture: Shortcut Check

Take your putting setup, then take your right hand off the putter grip and relax your arm, allowing it to hang. If you are properly bent forward from your hips, your hand should remain hanging by this side of the grip of the putter. If when you allow your right arm to hang it moves closer to you and inside of your putter grip, first check to see that your posture is proper, with your rear end pushed back and a minimal knee flex. If you bend your knees too much, your rear end will tuck under and your back will round out incorrectly. When this happens, it often puts the chest in the way and will not allow the arms to swing freely and independently from the body. If this does not correct the problem, you will need to step farther from your putter. If you stand too close to the golf ball it is not necessary to bend forward from your hips, and this makes it much harder to get into proper posture.

If when you let your right arm hang it moves away from you and outside of the putter grip, you will need to step in closer. Step in to the point where your hand is naturally hanging next to the grip of the putter and then place it onto the grip.

## Ladies, Does Your Putter Even Fit You?

Unless you have had your putter cut down, fitted especially for you, or you are quite tall (five-foot-nine or taller), your putter probably does not fit you. If your putter is too long, and most are, it is nearly impossible to get into the proper posture unless you place your hands onto the shaft of the putter below the grip.

Bend forward from you hips so that you feel like you are bowing forward and your chest is over your toes. As you let your arms naturally hang, place your hands onto the putter no matter where they fall, even if they are below the rubber grip of the putter. This would be the proper length of the putter for you, plus and inch or two to make room for the grip of the putter. Most women find that their putters are too long. The difference in the results with a putter that fits can be dramatic as well, making it possible to move only your arms and shoulders, rather than your entire body. I am five-foot-seven and my putter has been cut to thirty-one inches, which is five inches shorter than the length it was when it was purchased. You can check with your professional to see if your putter fits you properly or needs to be shortened.

If your putting posture is correct, a relaxed right arm will hang right next to the putter grip.

## Aiming the Face

Especially on your shorter putts, you'll need to be exact in your ability to aim the putter face. This often needs to be practiced to be good. You probably already have a feel for your ability to aim your putter face by whether you are confident in making your shorter putts.

## Aiming the Face: Shortcut Check—Use a Chalk Line

A great way to aim your putter face is to practice with a chalk line. If you've never seen one, it is an inexpensive carpentry tool that uses chalk to snap a straight line between two points. You

Snap down a chalk line to help aim your putter face.

can purchase one at any home improvement store for less than fifteen dollars. If you wish to improve your short putting, in my opinion this is the best way.

Find a straight putt of approximately five to six feet. Snap down a chalk line. Practice putting three- to five-footers by placing your golf ball onto the chalk line, paying special attention to your putter face keeping it perpendicular to the chalk line. If your putter has a line to help you to aim, make sure that it matches the chalk line exactly.

Your short-cut check is to aim the putter face to your target properly by matching the line on your putter to the chalk line, completely setting up, and then looking to your target. Does it look like it usually does? Or does it look different, like it would without the aid of the line on the ground? If it looks the same, you are probably good at aiming the face. If looks little off, you will probably need to continue your practice on the line to learn to train your eye.

When I practice on a chalk line the putter face will often appear slightly too far left to me, but after years of practice I have learned that for me, this is correct. If I am preparing to play a competitive round I will always spend some of my practice time on a chalk line. I do not use a lot of training aids when I teach, but this one is terrific and well worth your investment and your time.

## Aiming the Face: Quick Tip—Use the Writing on Your Golf Ball

To help you to aim your putter face you can use the writing on your golf ball. Mark your golf ball on the green, standing directly behind the ball, so that your golf ball is between you and your target, then aim, using the writing on your golf ball to your target. If it is a straight putt, aim the wording straight. If it is a right-to-left putt, aim the writing to the right, the amount you think the ball will curve, and do the reverse for a left-to-right putt. Keep in mind that other than on severely fast or undulated greens you would not want to aim the wording outside of the cup for your short putts. Once you aim the wording to your target you should take a couple of steps back away from the ball to survey your work. You can only truly survey the line from a couple of steps back behind your golf ball because being too close can distort the view. If it looks good, you should then remove your marker. If it looks incorrect, make the necessary adjustments and then remove your marker. You should always take this extra time to do this to double-check, confirming that you have aimed the wording properly.

After you take your practice stroke aim the putter face so that the line on the putter

Aim the writing on your golf ball to help you to aim your putter face.

Left: Stand behind your golf ball to double check the line is aimed properly.

Above: Use a permanent marker to help you to see the line more clearly.

matches the line on the ball exactly. If you do not have an aiming line on your putter, you might consider changing putters to one that does have a line, or having one added to your putter. Any club-repair shop should be able to do this for a reasonable cost as well as cut your putter shorter if necessary. Once you have matched the putter line to the wording line of the ball, you should then set your feet so the line across your toes is parallel to your intended target line.

 If you have any trouble seeing the line of the wording, you can always take a permanent marker and extend the line to make it more obvious. Using the wording to help aim the putter face is completely legal and a very popular method. I use it on almost every putt. I'm reading your mind: no, it should not take too long. With a little practice using this method you can become very quick and efficient. If it does take too long you can practice this process to become quicker. And by taking fewer putts, you'll save time. So, take the time and make the effort, and slow your life down for five seconds and watch your scores drop as your confidence soars.

## Aiming the Face: Quick Tip—The "Nancy Lopez" Method

Another method of helping you to aim your putter face is made very popular by Nancy Lopez. Stand behind your golf ball so that it is directly between you and your target. Then set the putter head behind the ball and aim the face on your intended target line. Since you are standing behind the ball you'll have a direct view of your target line and not the distortion you would see when standing to the side. Like throwing a dart or hitting a pool shot, you can see the line better from behind. Think how difficult it would be to throw a dart straight to your target standing sidesaddle. This distortion is also much like the one you see on television due to the angle of the camera relative to the golfer. Because it would be inappropriate for the camera person to stand directly behind the golfer, the angle at which the ball appears to leave the club often looks very crooked. This is also the reason why the camera angle needs to be exact when you are working with video to help your golf game.

Once you aim the face properly to your target, be very careful not to let it move or change its position even slightly. Walk

Use the "Nancy Lopez" method to help to aim your putter face.

around to the side of the ball, set your hands to the grip of the putter, and then set your feet, making sure that the line through your toes is parallel to the aiming line on your putter. This method will only work if you are able to keep the putter face aiming where you originally set it as you walk around to set your hands and then your feet. One of my students, Cheryl, after too many missed short putts, chose to adopt this Nancy Lopez style of aiming her putter face. Since making this change, Cheryl's putting has gone from less than satisfactory to very respectable. Her extra time and care is absolutely being rewarded.

### The Push Drill for Better Short Putting: Quick Tip

Your putting stroke should be the same length back and through, or slightly longer forward than back. If you tend to stop your forward stroke, rather than properly keeping your arms and the putter moving forward, it can be difficult to consistently sink those shorter test putts. The push drill will help teach you to make a proper forward stroke. Find a three- to five-foot putt and take your setup. Make absolutely no backstroke and practice pushing your golf ball to the hole. This can help teach you the importance of the forward stroke, the control that it has on the putter face, your ability to make these putts. While it might feel a little odd at first, you will be amazed how many putts you can make with just a forward stroke. Unfortunately, this is not a legal stroke, but it is a great way to train yourself to keep your arms and putter moving forward so that your forward stroke is as long if not slightly longer than your backstroke.

## Putting—Putter Face Aiming and Distance Control

Just as aiming the face of your putter was the absolute most important fundamental for your short putts, distance control will be the most important for all other putts. To control the distance that you roll the ball when you putt, you'll want to vary the size of the stroke you make. When you need more distance you should make a larger stroke, which should naturally have more speed due to the larger pendulum. Keep in mind that the stroke should be the same length back and throughout or slightly longer on the forward stroke. While practice and experience are often the reasons for the ability to control distance, there are fundamentals for success and methods you can apply immediately to help improve your game.

Controlling your distance will be much easier if you can limit the number of moving parts. The triangle formed between your arms and shoulders should move as a pendulum so that your shoulders rock in a teeter-totter motion. This should be all that moves. Your lower body should not move at all. While there are good players who do break their wrists while putting, I think it is preferable that you do not.

## Distance Control: Shortcut Check— No Lower-Body Movement

Complete your putting stroke and hold your finish. This will give you opportunity to see if your lower body has maintained its original position by checking to see that your hips are still facing forward in the direction of the ball at address and also to check to see that your knees have not moved or turned. If they have incorrectly moved, your right knee will often move closer toward the target.

## Distance Control: Quick Tip— No Lower-Body Movement

To assist in keeping your lower body absolutely still, you can pigeon-toe your feet. This will limit your flexibility and make it much more difficult to move your lower body, even if you try. The more you turn in your toes, the less you are able to turn. You

Pigeon-toe your feet to keep your lower body still.

can use this for practice and or you can absolutely use it when you play. Arnold Palmer often did this when he putted.

You may find that to keep your lower body completely still requires a conscious effort. Because it is OK for your lower body to move in all of your other swings and strokes, this restriction makes putting different. Spend part of your practice time consciously thinking about keeping your lower body completely still and see if this feels different to you. If it does, you will need to spend a part of your practice time thinking consciously about this.

### Distance Control: Quick Tip— Minimize Wrist Movement

If you feel your wrists tend to move too much, try holding the putter more firmly with your left hand. The firmer the grip, the less likely the wrists are to "break down."

### Distance Control: Quick Tip—To Minimize Your Wrists from Breaking Down, Try Left Hand Low

A very popular style of putting today is called left hand low. This is where the hands are reversed on the grip of the putter so that the left hand is lower than the right. The purpose for the origination of left hand low was to make easier to keep the left wrist flat throughout the putting stroke. I think it has valid reasons for working, and you can use it to help you become a less "wristy" putter. There are three ways you might use left hand low. You can use it as a practice drill. To help you to feel less wrist movement, roll some practice putts with this grip, being aware of how a flat left wrist feels. You can also use left hand low as a kinesthetic prompt during your preparation before you putt your golf ball. I will often use this method if I feel my wrists are moving too much. During your round of golf you can make your practice strokes left and low to help you to feel constant wrist angles, then return to your normal grip right before you putt. This will help to give you the proper feel right before you make the stroke that really counts.

You might also find that this method in your practice or your preshot preparation actually results in better putting. If so, you may choose to use this as your overall putting style. If you struggle with your distance control, it is always worth trying. My student, Victor, was not a very good putter, which even he would admit. We then introduced him to the left-hand-low method and his putting has dramatically improved. And while he still never takes the time and care that I would like, it certainly is much more respectable.

Try left hand low to minimize wrist movement.

## Distance Control: Quick Tip—
## Like Rolling a Ball

Stand right next to your golf ball facing the hole. How far would you need to swing your arm back and through if you were going to roll the ball there? You'll be amazed how close this can be to the size stroke you will need. My college teammate at Furman University, Margaret Will, who plays on the LPGA tour, used this method quite successfully. By pretending to roll a ball the appro-

Pretend to roll a ball to help with distance control.

priate distance with your arm you receive terrific input into the stroke size needed with a motion you already know.

### Distance Control: Quick Tip— Assign the Point Value from 1 to 15

This system is very general, but can really serve to help if you struggle with what size putting stroke is necessary for differing distances. There are no exacts here, so you might have to use some of your own creativity. One of my students, Paul, lacks depth perception due to a vision problem, and we developed this system to help give him a sense of the size stroke and power that he needs.

If a point value of 1 is your shortest stroke and 15 is your largest stroke, you can assign a point value to each putt by determining approximately how large a stroke is needed. This system will take into account the length of the putt as well as uphill versus downhill and fast versus slow greens.

The first step is to assess the overall length of the putt and rate it between 1 for a very, very short putt, and 11 for the longest putt you've ever had. You then adjust for the undulation. If the putt is a little uphill, add a point. If it is severely uphill, add two. Conversely, if the putt is downhill, subtract one point for slightly, and two for severely downhill. You can also add or subtract for particularly slow or fast greens. For a little slower green add one point, and for very slow add two. On faster greens, subtract one for slightly faster and subtract two for U.S. Open speed greens. This will give you an idea of the size of stroke you need. While this system is not exact, it does require you to assess the situation and make a decision about approximately how large a putting stroke is needed.

For example, if you have a fifteen-foot putt you might give it a rating of 4 in distance, another point for being a little uphill so you add 1, and another point because of slower greens, making the putt a 6. While I do not necessarily need to assign an exact size stroke for my 6-putt out of a possible fifteen, it still gives me an idea of how large a stroke and how much energy I will need to roll the ball the right distance.

## Distance Control: Quick Tip—
## Really Fast "Lightning" Putt

Have you ever had one of those putts that looked so fast you were scared to stroke it, like if you were just to breathe on it, it would be too much? In these cases try gripping extremely low on the putter. Hold below the grip and onto the shaft. It may feel a little strange, but try it. The shorter putter will automatically deliver less power to the ball due to the shorter lever. I am surprised that more golfers do not use this technique. I showed it to one of my students at Atlantic right before our big member-guest tournament. Our greens are always amazing during this tournament because our superintendent, Bob Ranum, makes the course a showcase especially for this event, and the greens are like ice. My student put this technique to use, survived the greens, and won his flight. Part of my job as a golf instructor is to prepare my students for this type of situation. By having the experience of playing a relatively high level of tournament golf, I feel I have the ability to help my students to get ready for their competitive endeavors.

Hold very low on your putter on extremely fast putts.

## *Chip and Bump and Run*

A chip and bump and run are virtually the same shot. The only difference is that a chip will land onto the green when it comes out of the air and then run more than it carried, while the bump and run will land short of the green when it initially comes out of the air and then roll to the target. Both shots are referred to as chipping in this section to keep it more simple. If you can putt, you can chip. While the setup is different, the stroke is exactly the same.

Chipping setup and motion.

### A Quick Chipping /Bump-and-Run Review

- A higher percentage of the distance is rolling.

- Grip down and step in closer.

- Keep your stance narrow.

- Weight starts, stays, and finishes on your left.

- Ball position centered to slightly right of center in your stance.

- The motion is like that of a putting stroke that sweeps the grass.

- Control the percentage of roll or the total distance with your club selection.

Here are two important chipping concepts:

## Different Ball Position Option

Your ball position affects trajectory and therefore the amount of roll. When you chip you have the option of playing the ball centered in your stance or, if you prefer, farther back in your stance, closer to being in line it with the big toe on your right foot. Since your stance is quite narrow for chipping this is not a huge difference, but it is one you need to understand. The more you play the ball in line with your right foot, the more your ball will roll relative to a center ball position. This should be easy to remember by thinking "right foot for roll."

## Different Club Selection Options

You can use many of your clubs to chip or just a couple of favorites—your choice. Choose the appropriate club based upon the percentage of roll needed.

Or, you can choose to use just a couple of clubs. For example, you might use your pitching wedge when you need a little more roll than carry (⅓ carry and ⅔ roll) and you might use your 7 iron when you need a much higher percentage of roll. While this system may sound too simple, it would probably be the one I would recommend to a newer golfer. The advantage of using more of your clubs (sand wedge, pitching wedge, 9 iron, 8 iron, and 7 iron) is you can simply learn one basic chipping stroke and change the club, depending upon how much roll you need.

How do you know if you are chipping correctly? Here are some shortcut checks:

✔ **Chipping Posture: Shortcut Check—Right Arm Hanging**

When you grip lower on your club for chipping you should also step in closer to maintain proper posture and be in balance. If you grip lower and do not step in closer you will be bent over too much and out of balance. Besides making it much more difficult to accomplish repetitive, solid contact, this grip would be tough on your lower back. First, check your posture, as you did for your full swing and for putting. Take your complete setup, then take your right hand off the grip, relax your arm completely, and let it hang. If your posture and distance from the ball are correct, your hand should remain next to the grip of the club as you let your arm hang. If your arm moves away from the grip of the club and closer to you, first check that you have not bent your knees too much. It should still be possible to feel that your rear end is pushed back. If this does not correct the problem, it might be necessary for you to step closer to the ball to the point where your relaxed right arm places your right hand next to the grip of the club.

Take your right hand off the grip of the club and allow the arm to hang. If it moves away from you and outside of the grip, you are probably standing too close and it will be necessary to back your feet away to the point where your hand hangs right next to the grip of the club.

These setup and posture checks are quick and painless, something you can use during your round for reassurance, especially if you are having trouble with balance or contact. It is such a simple method, I highly doubt that others playing with you would even notice.

## Chipping Stance Width: Shortcut Check

You know your stance should be narrow for chipping. This is to make it easier for you to keep your weight on your left foot throughout the stroke. Your stance for chipping should be no wider at your heels than the width of your club head. You can place your club head, sideways, between your heels intermittently to check and maintain a consistent width.

## The Chipping Motion: Shortcut Checks— Hold Your Finish

As chipping and putting are virtually the same motion, it is important that you generate the stroke by using your arms rather than your wrists. You can check this by holding your finish to see whether your forearms have both moved to the left side of your body. You can also check your finish to see whether your club head is still relatively low to the ground when you finish your stroke. Because your weight is on your left foot, the club head should finish lower to the ground as a result of your left shoulder being lower than your right due to the leaning of your weight to the left.

You can also check your finish to see whether you have used your forearms correctly by seeing whether your left arm and the shaft of the club are still in a line. Hold your finish and then

Your chipping stance should be a club head apart at your heels.

To check your chipping finish remove your right hand and see that the club shaft and your left arm form a straight line.

remove your right hand from the grip of a club to see the left arm and club shaft form a straight line. This will also help the club head to finish lower to the ground. You can also check your finish to see that your weight is still on your left foot. You should easily be able to pick up your right heel without needing to shift your weight. I have seen Mike Adams use a technique to teach his students how to keep the club low to the ground past the golf ball. He places his foot, heel down and toes up, with toes a few inches above the ball, and tells his student, "Don't hit my foot." While Mike is a little more brave than I am, I think it is a terrific idea, and I have done the same thing with a golf club. One of my students has always struggled with his chipping and he had just purchased two new, beautiful, shiny wedges. As he practiced his chipping, I took one of the two new clubs and placed it just over the top of his golf ball and told him to not hit his club. Several times he made his usual mistake of trying to lift the golf ball, smashing his two new wedges together, and then he got the point. He then started keeping the club head lower to the ground and hitting nice, crisp chips. His chipping got significantly better afterwards, and I am sorry that I had not used this technique sooner.

You've used your shortcut checks and found some shortcomings. Use the following quick tips to help you to make the necessary corrections:

Take your chipping practice stroke with your putter and your putting motion.

Change to the club you will use and repeat the same putting motion.

## The Chipping Motion: Quick Tip—
## Using Your Forearms Correctly

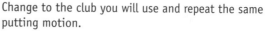

As you already know, putting and chipping are the same motion with different setups. You can use your putter to help to improve your chipping, in practice or for your on-course preshot preparation. If you struggle with your chipping, I promise this will help. By using a motion you probably already know, you can shorten the learning curve. Take a practice stroke for your chip shot with your putter. Remember that your putting stroke should be the same length back and through, and to accomplish this your arms and the putter must continue moving forward. Make an actual putting setup and stroke. Then switch to the club you will use to chip. The only adjustment you'll make is to lean left. You will not make another practice stroke. Then repeat what you felt with your putter while your weight remains left.

## Long Back-and-Stop Does Not Work

When you chip, if you make too long of a back stroke and then stop, you will not be a good chipper. I see this all the time. There is a very specific order for improvement. The first step is that you must teach yourself to follow through for at least as long as you take the club back. When you first begin to follow through properly, your golf ball will very likely travel too far. This is both good and necessary in order to improve and make the needed changes. If you are following though properly but your ball is traveling too far, you can then make the necessary adjustment of shortening your backstroke to keep the golf ball from traveling too far.

Long back-and-stop does not work because whatever distance your arms and club swing back, you have generated an equal amount of potential momentum on the other side. When you attempt to stop this momentum on the forward swing by stopping your arms, the club head still has momentum and will keep going, causing your wrists to "break down." This will make both distance and particularly direction control very difficult.

If this sounds like something that you might be doing in your chipping, say to yourself every time you chip, "Shorter back and longer through." Say it over and over until you see that your chipping stroke becomes the same length back and through without this mantra. The skill might take quite some time, so it cannot hurt to put this positive thought into your head.

## The Chipping Motion: Quick Tip—
## Using Your Forearms Correctly

To teach you to keep your arms moving forward on your chipping motion you can use the following kinesthetic drill. It will help you to feel the necessarily flat left wrist throughout your forward stroke. Place your hands very low on the shaft of the club so that your hands are only eight to twelve inches from the club head. Allow the shaft of the club to point to the left of you, on the left side of your body. Make your chipping motion, being sure that the shaft of the club maintains its distance away from your rib cage. If your arms stop, the shaft of the club will hit against your rib cage and probably be uncomfortable. If your arms move properly forward, if should be quite easy to maintain the relationship of the shaft away from your rib cage.

## The Chipping Motion: Quick Tip— Using Your Forearms Correctly

When you place your hands low on the grip of the club, place the handle into the left sleeve of your sweater or jacket. As you make a chipping stroke with your arms the handle should remain comfortably in the sleeve. If you do not move your arms properly or try to overuse your wrist, you'll find this very difficult.

To use your forearms correctly when chipping, hold low on the handle and maintain the grip position in the left sleeve of your sweater.

Practice chipping with your right heel up to help keep your weight to stay left.

## Weight Left for Chipping: Quick Tip— Right Heel Up

Your weight should start, stay, and finish on your left foot when chipping. This also helps to decrease the loft of the club face and produce the desired greater percentage of roll. You can use it in practice or for your actual chip shot, as it is another of those little tips that is so unobtrusive that others in your group might not even notice. You can even use it in play, if you chose. Take your practice stroke for your chips with your right heel off the ground throughout the stroke. This will insure that your weight stays left, producing a more descending angle of attack, which makes it easier for the club to brush the ground after the ball. When you first try this it may feel too exaggerated, but you will find that your contact with the ball becomes much more solid and crisp, with practice. However exaggerated your weight on your left feels in this drill is how much you should feel even when your heel is down.

## *Pitching*

While the pitch shot is your last short-game option, it is a very important shot, one that might be more demanding of proper fundamentals and practice time.

## Quick Pitching Review

- More carry than roll.

- Use your sand wedge.

- Center the ball position.

- The end of the club points to the belly button.

- Swing size controls distance.

- Setup helps to control swing size.

- Swing size the same length back and through.

- The bottom of the golf club must brush grass to get the golf ball into the air at proper height.

## The Bounce

If this is a new golf word or idea to you, I really want you to read this section twice because it is important and I have seen most women using it incorrectly. One of my ladies in the short-game clinic said it best: "Square looks open." That's it! I could not have said it better. Square looks open. When you set your sand wedge properly, it does look open.

When you set your sand wedge properly on its bounce it may appear open to you.

The bounce is the rounded bottom of the club, and it is specific to a sand wedge and a lob wedge, if you choose to carry one. If you set the sand wedge properly when you address the ball, the face might look open to you. This is correct and will allow the rounded bottom to skim the ground rather than incorrectly dig-

If your sand wedge digs excessively, you are probably not using the bounce correctly.

ging. If you hit the ground with your sand wedge, making giant divots, the bounce is probably the issue. It is the forgiveness design, enabling the bottom of the club to glide across the ground and react like a rock skipping across water. As long as the rock's rounded flat side hits the water all is well, but what happens when the edge of the rock catches the water? It abruptly stops and sinks. As long as you address the ball correctly, using the bounce, the sand wedge should not dig, which makes it much more difficult to hit a fat pitch shot. If you are not afraid to hit fat, you are less likely to be hesitant to hit the ground and less likely to hit skulls.

### Pitching Setup: Shortcut Check— Are You Setting the Club Properly on Its Bounce? The Concrete Test

You can check to see that you are using the bounce properly when you set up and swing, by taking a small pitch swing and allowing the bottom of the club to hit a solid surface. You could use a painted board or a gravel path. Keep in mind: the harder the surface, the smaller the swing you should take to avoid injury or excessive damage to your sand wedge. You must hit the bottom of the club on the surface hard enough to mark the club. If you are setting the club properly, the trailing edge is where the contact should show, not the leading edge.

The concrete test identifies if the bounce is being used properly.

## Pitching/Bounce Setup: Shortcut Check— "Thump" the Ground

You can also check to see if you are setting your sand wedge properly by taking some small swings and really letting the club thump the ground. If the sand wedge is set properly it should not dig or take extra-large chunks of turf. While it might make a mark in the ground, it should not be digging and stopping. This should also be a part of your preparation to hit a pitch shot during your round. Along with deciding the necessary swing and setup size, I also want to feel and hear my sand wedge "thump" the ground a few times before the actual shot.

## Pitching/Bounce Setup: Quick Tip— Use the Hidden Markings on Your Golf Club

Your golf club will often have markings, however small and unnoticeable, to help you to set the club properly on the ground. Once you are aware of them, you can use them, to help you. Your club may or may not have these:

This "tick" mark should set on the top of the grip when your club is soled properly.

- a small "tick" mark on the top of the bottom of the grip of the club. Assuming that the grip is installed correctly on your club, this mark should sit on the top of the grip, without favoring either side when the club is soled properly. Most golfers are unaware of these marks and are often surprised when I show them it is there to help them to set up properly.

- writing on the shaft—many golf clubs will have this. Most often, but not always, the writing should sit on the top of the shaft, without favoring either side when the club is soled properly.

### Pitching Motion: Quick Tip—Piggyback Drill

When you pitch the ball, the swing should be the same length back and through. In order for you to do this, your arms should swing as far forward as they do back. If you do it properly, your lead arm should continue swinging forward. To train yourself to do this you can use the piggyback drill. I thought it was terrific when I watched Mr. Bob Toski use it. Hold very low on the grip of your sand wedge with your left hand to keep the club from feeling excessively heavy. Piggyback your right hand on top of your left so that no part of your right hand touches the grip of the club. Don't try to cheat and cheat yourself—no part of your right hand should touch the grip of the club, your right hand should completely rest on the top of your left. Practice swinging your left arm back and through as your right hand rests on top, just along

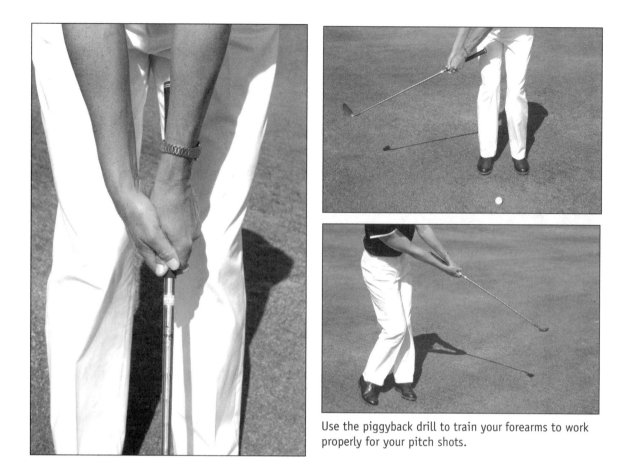

Use the piggyback drill to train your forearms to work properly for your pitch shots.

for the ride. This will train your lead arm to keep moving and minimize the chance that you might try to lift or scoop your golf ball. You can do this drill while hitting golf balls, usually with a small pitching motion. One of my students was a much better pitcher of the golf ball when she did this piggyback drill, rather than the normal, so we switched her to the piggyback method for her short pitches during her on-course play.

## Pitching Distance Control: Quick Tip—Use Your Setup

Control your distance when you pitch with your swing size, and control your swing size with your setup. I've seen tremendous improvement using this system, and it always surprises me that

For your small pitch shot, place your hands to the bottom of the grip and narrow your stance to where your feet are together.

more golfers do not know or use it. I learned it from Mike Adams, when I had the privilege to teach with him at PGA National in Palm Beach Gardens, Florida.

The shorter the distance you need to pitch the ball, the smaller the setup you should have. Control your set up by where you place your hands on the grip of the club (high or low) and by the width of your stance (hip width to feet touching). For your smallest pitch shots you should place your hands at the bottom of the grip of the club and narrow your stance to the point that your feet are touching. By holding very low on the grip, you shorten the lever and therefore the power. By narrowing your stance you limit your flexibility and therefore the possible length of your backswing. If you have never tried this it is going to feel very strange at first, but I think it will make enough difference in your ability to control your distance that you should be able to move past that feeling. As you need greater distance and a larger swing, your setup should get proportionally larger, your hands should

For a larger pitch shot, your hands should be higher on the grip and your feet should be wider, allowing your swing to get larger.

get higher, and your feet should get wider. You can use this system and be very basic. For example, you could learn a small, medium, and large pitch with a setup size that matches the desired swing size. Or you could be more exact and match a setup to a desired distance. You might learn what setup is needed to produce a ten-yard, a twenty-yard, a thirty-yard, and a forty-yard pitch shot for you. If you knew what setup you needed for each of these distances, it would be much easier to reproduce these distances upon demand during your golf round.

## Pitching, Putting, and Practice

Maybe it is not an accident that both pitching and putting start with the letter *P*, because they both require practice to be successful. When you practice your putting and pitching you should first start by checking your fundamentals and then transition into improving your feel by working on your distance control. Hitting one or two good pitches or putts does not end your practice session. As you improve, try to narrow the parameters that are acceptable, or increase the number of good shots in a row that you need to hit before you can move on.

## Greenside Bunker

The greenside bunker is often the stumbling block for a lot of women. Due to lower club-head speed, it can be difficult to throw the sand far enough out of the bunker so that the ball will come out with the sand.

### Quick Bunker Review

The goal is to throw the sand out of the bunker and the ball will travel with it. The club head should never touch the golf ball. The sand will act as a buffer between the club head and the golf ball, so a very full golf swing will be necessary. Your setup will help you to be able to take sand.

- **Ball position left in stance to help you to contact the sand before the ball.**

- **Hand position high on grip to help you to take sand.**

- **Dig your feet into the sand to lower the bottom of your golf swing and to help you to take sand.**

- **Take a full swing with a full finish, where your right heel comes up to the toes as a result of the full swing.**

- **Control your distance with your swing speed.**

### You and I Are Not Tiger!

I realize that this is not big news for most of us. My ego is not even slightly bruised by the fact that little of what I consider good golf resembles what Tiger Woods is able to do, or even Annika

The greenside bunker requires the proper setup and a full swing.

Sorenstam, for that matter. Annika played in a men's PGA tour event this year and handled herself with such class that I was endlessly impressed. Due to a string of rainy days in the Northeast, I was able to watch most of her golf shots during her two days. And while she did not make the cut, she set a good example for all athletes, male or female, in any sport.

The point here is that, since we are not Tiger or Annika and absolutely do not launch the golf ball, a lot of the inappropriate advice that we are receiving comes from those who think that they can. Most women do not need to open their club face in the bunker. Because we generate less club-head speed, an open club face will only make the ball travel shorter, and since the sand acts as a buffer already between the club head and the ball, shorter is not a necessary option. Because the club face is not open, the body does not need to be open. The only reason a golfer may want to open his or her body more in the bunker is to compensate for the club face, aiming more to the right when it is opened.

If Tiger or Annika opens the club face to hit the golf ball higher and shorter, they need to walk around the alignment circle to realign the club face to the target. And since you probably do not need to open the face, you probably do not need to open your body. This serves to dispel many of the myths of the bunker that are being passed along and confusing the heck out of us.

How do you know if what you're doing is correct? Use the following tests to help determine whether you are:

✔ **Greenside Bunker: Shortcut Check—
Can You Throw Out the Sand?**

Can you throw the sand out of the bunker? We're not talking about a couple of granules, but rather a very large cloud of sand. Practice throwing sand out of the bunker without a golf ball. Can you generate enough speed to successfully throw the sand of the bunker and onto the green? If you are unable to throw the sand out of the bunker, do not attempt to add a golf ball until you can. One of my students, Lynne, needs all her might to get her golf ball out of the bunker. With a little cheerleading, she has learned to hit some absolutely beautiful bunker shots, but she has to motivate herself each time to get to this high level of exertion.

✔ **Greenside Bunker: Shortcut Check—Check Your Finish**

Can you tap your right toe when you hold your finish? Is the shaft of the golf club still over your left shoulder? Hit a splash bunker shot and hold your finish. Check to see that you can tap your right toe without having to falsely add more turn or more ✔ weight transfer. Also check to see that your club shaft taps your left shoulder at this finish position. This position should be a natural result of your swing speed. If your arms swing with enough speed, a finish is a result and not a conscious effort.

If you fail to accomplish either of these shortcut checks, try the following quick tips to help you to improve the full swing necessary to be successful with your green-side bunker shots.

### ⏱ Bunker Play: Quick Tip—Throwing the Sand and the Ball out of the Bunker

If you were unable to throw the sand far enough on of the bunker you should first check to see that your sand wedge face is properly, allowing the bounce to work for you. As mentioned earlier, the face might look open to you when set correctly, as it is the most lofted club many of us carry. Once this is correct, then gain a little attitude. Imagine that sand is one of your least favorite people and really throw that sand out of the bunker. For golfers with lower club-head speed this often takes a lot more speed and swing then you would initially think.

In a greenside bunker, you should go to a full finish.

### ⏱ Bunker Play: Quick Tip—Scrape Drill to Finish, Tap Toe and Shoulder

To learn to take sand and to go to a full finish in the greenside bunker, practice a scrape drill to a full finish. Take your setup, with or without a golf ball, but take no backswing. Scrape the sand in a semicircle, curving left, and go to a full finish where your right foot rotates up to the toes in reaction to your rotating body. The shaft of your sand wedge should rest on your left shoulder at your finish position. The club head should scrape the sand for at least ten to twelve inches. This will help you to feel the club head cut a path through the sand and the proper finish needed to generate enough speed to hit successful splash bunker shots. Once you are successful with the drill, add a backswing and

The scrape drill will teach you to take a long patch of sand in the bunker.

momentum, but maintain the feeling of this scrape drill on the forward swing. The longer the length of your divot in the sand the better bunker player you will be. If your divot is eight to twelve inches long, as long as your golf ball is anywhere within this divot it should come out of the bunker with the sand, provided you have enough momentum to throw the sand the appropriate distance.

 **Splash the Sand out of the Bunker: Quick Tip—
Erase the Footprint**

To help you to practice taking a longer path of sand out of the bunker, I learned a trick from my fellow golf instructor, Jeff Warne, at Atlantic. Make a footprint in the practice bunker. Take your setup and bunker swing, then practice taking out the entire footprint. This teaches you to take a longer path of sand out of the bunker and it gives you more of a margin for error and more successful bunker shots.

## Splash the Sand out of the Bunker: Quick Tip— Throw the Rocks or Tees Out

To help you to throw the sand out of the bunker with enough momentum, you can first learn to throw out either rocks or golf tees. If you are successful in throwing these out with the sand, when you add the golf ball with the same intent you will have success. When I took my LPGA Teaching and Club Professional class-A testing I had to give a bunker lesson, and I used the throw-the-tee-out demonstration. My student did very well and I was pleased to receive my class-A status.

# Strategy

7

Strategy becomes an important part of lowering your score. Once you have proficient skills and are aware of the techniques that you can apply, they often seem obvious in hindsight, but if you apply them they will help you to play smarter golf. Your strategy and ability to adjust your game plan throughout your round can and will determine the success of your score. Some days you will hit the ball better than others. That is just a simple fact. But by adjusting your game plan to the skills you have that day, you will still be able to lower your scores.

## Learn to Adjust Your Game Plan
## Throughout Your Round

You must constantly be assessing your performance. On the good ball-striking days you'll allow yourself to graduate to your more demanding clubs and to be more aggressive in taking dead aim at the pins on the greens. On the not-so-fun days when you are not hitting the ball solidly, it is so very important that you play more conservatively. It is really important to play more "chicken" when you are not hitting the ball well. Examples of playing more conservatively in these instances include:

1. Teeing off with a physically shorter club, for example, a 5 wood instead of a driver. By using a physically shorter club you should automatically experience a higher success rate, and the increased loft will help you to hit the ball straighter, due to lesser side spin.

2. Using a more lofted fairway wood for your distance shots, for example, a 7 wood instead of a 5 wood. For the same reasons that teeing off with a physically shorter club could help you experience more success, the shorter club and the increased loft should help you to experience more success on your fairway shots.

3. Playing around the trouble—choosing to bump and run or chip to the openings of the green rather than pitching over the bunker. Because you will require a smaller swing when chipping than when pitching, the risk of a poor result is that much less. And if by chance you do not quite hit the ground enough, there is still a good chance that the ball might roll up and onto the putting surface because there is nothing to go over.

What do you do on the days when your swing seems to totally fail you? I'm sure you've had one of these. We all have. I remember playing a qualifying round in college when it was so cold it was sleeting. I could barely make contact. I resorted to hitting half swing, five irons to complete my round. While my score was higher than I would have liked, by completely changing my game plan to adjust to the conditions and my lack of ability that day, at least I was able to complete my round and post a score. So, do you have a backup plan for when your golf swing fails? If not, you should.

A very viable option when your swing fails is to take a smaller swing with a longer club. For example, you might be your normal 7-iron distance from your target, but choose to take a smaller swing with a 6 iron instead. The smaller the swing, the less chance for error, and this adjustment may be enough to successfully get you through the round. On the driving range, practice taking less than full swings with longer clubs. You may be surprised by this success rate.

## More Difficult Holes

Every golf course has them—those few holes that are much more difficult than the others. You might have your own select few that seem to jump up and get you. These in particular are the holes where strategy is important, where you want to play more conservatively and have a definite plan of attack. For example, if there is a par 4 that is particularly long, 390 yards, would you think this hole were easier if it were a par 5 at 410 yards? If the design of the hole is the same but 20 yards longer, its reasonable to think it is more difficult. But when it's a par 5, is it easier? No, is the answer. So, if you were to change your state of mind and think of the 390-yard hole as an easier par 5, that might be a better plan with a higher success rate.

If you press to achieve more it often leads to failure. If you can adjust your mind-set and your game plan I think you'll find more success. The couple of times that I have been able to play Shinnecock Hills in Long Island, I adjusted my game plan to play several of the par 4s like par 5s because they were so long and difficult. A lot of the older golf courses where they have not set appropriate tees for women are like this, so they will play very long. The newer golf course are built with the distances that women do hit the golf ball a little more in mind.

## Personal Par

Try assigning your own personal par in a game plan for these more difficult holes. You can determine your personal par by figuring out how many average shots it will take you to get on or around the green, then add two for the putting. We're not talking your absolute best, perfect shots, but your regular, comfortable distance.

### Calculating Personal Par

390-yard hole

Average tee shot: 140 yards

Average fairway wood: 120 yards

One tee shot: 140 yards

Two fairway woods: 240 yards (2 X 120)

Total yardage = 380 yards

One ten-yard short-game shot

Four shots plus two putts equals a personal par of six

If you hit a great tee shot and two great fairway woods you might be able to get there in three and hopefully score lower than your personal par on your A-plus golf day, but rather than pressing and being disappointed, the reasonable goal of a personal par 6 will help to lower your score. The better way to lower your score in this case would be to play to your present skill level, get to the green in four and sharpen your short-game skills—to hit the short-game shot close enough to the pin and to one-putt and score one less than your own personal par.

## Tee Shot Strategy

You've heard the old saying "Drive for show and putt for dough." While I do agree with the importance of the putting, there sure is something to be said about hitting successful tee shots. Along with the positive mental boost a good drive can give you, a good drive can set the stage for your success. Your drive does not need to be heroic, just reliable and effective.

Other than your setup and swing fundamentals, the most important decision for your tee shots is the club you select. You should use a club you can actually hit with consistency, one in which you also have confidence. I don't care what club that is. If it's a 9 wood, it's a 9 wood. If it's a 3 wood, it's a 3 wood and so on. I watched one of my juniors, Cecilia, choose to tee off with her 9 iron and keep hitting with 9 irons down the fairway until the point where it was too much club. She was strong enough to be able to hit the ball a respectable distance and egoless enough to choose a club with which she was confident and had success with during her warm-up. She set a very good example for all of us.

The club you use to hit your tee ball will be determined in your preround warm-up. How are you striking the ball today? What was the longest club you were able to use with repetitive success on the range? Please don't get stuck in the old, "I should use a driver because I need the distance." I hear this all the time, and it is very common for women to get caught up in it. If you

Look for the most direct line to your target from the tee box.

do not generate enough club-head speed there is no advantage to using a driver other than peer pressure. If you are able to successfully and consistently (70 to 80 percent), tee off with your driver, then more power to you. But, if your level of success is lower than this, lose the attitude and use the club you can actually hit well. For the small amount distance you might sacrifice on the "perfect" golf swings you will more likely gain in effective, consistent tee shots. For many of my students who are just learning to play, we won't even order the longer woods until they are ready. There is nothing wrong with learning to get very good with your 9 and 7 woods first. I watched on of my students, Lainie, keep up with two very experienced golfers using her 7 wood to tee off and her 9 wood in the fairways. While she did hit slightly shorter than the others, she was very consistent and a couple of times kept up with the others on their tee shots with their drivers. Although Lainie did not have the experience, she faked it very well an had an extremely successful day. You can add the 5 wood when you are ready. And you can add the 3 wood when you are ready. And you can add the 1 wood when and if you are ever ready. It is much easier to not be tempted to hit these longer clubs if they are not even in your golf bag in the first place.

## Look for the Best Angle on Your Tee Shots

Once you've determined which club to use to tee off, you must then determine where to place your golf ball and tee within the teeing ground. Your legal teeing ground is a line across the tee markers extended two club lengths back. As you can see, it is an actual box, and as long as your golf ball is anywhere within and this area you are fine. When you are deciding where to place your tee into the ground, the first thing to look for is the best angle into your target, one that provides the least amount of obstacles. For example, you're playing a par 3 with a very large bunker on left side of the approach area to the green. If you were to tee off on the far right side of the tee box you would have a more direct line to the green without having to go over the bunker.

## Tee from the Side of the Trouble

The best angle into your target, provided it does not make you hit your golf ball over another obstacle, might be to tee off on the side of your trouble. While this might seem a little counterintuitive, it will make it easier to aim away from the obstacle. If there is an out-of-bounds on left side of the hole, it may be to your advantage to place the ball into the teeing ground on the left side. This will make it easier to aim to the right, away from the trouble.

I remember being a junior golfer at Seneca Lake Country Club in Geneva, New York, playing the sixteenth hole with out-of-bounds, all down the left side of the hole. The head golf professional, Phil Louvier, explained to me that I should tee off from the left side of the tee box, closer to the out-of-bounds, so that I would be able to aim away from the trouble. It made so much sense, once he opened my eyes to the idea, and it saved me many future penalty shots.

## Consider Your Natural Ball Flight

You'll also want to consider your natural ball flight when placing your ball on the tee box. This may also seem counterintuitive. If your ball tends to curve to the right, you'll want to tee your ball on the right side of the tee box, making it easier for you to aim to the left side of the fairway. If your ball flight remains straight you are still fine in the left side of the fairway. If your ball curves to the right, as it normally does, you'll have the entire fairway width, left to right, to work with, rather than just the half of fairway you would have if you aimed down the center. The reverse would be true if your predominant ball flight were right to left. If you tend to draw or hook the ball, you should tee off from the far left side of the tee box. This will make it easier to aim into the right side of the fairway, giving you the entire width of the fairway for the curvature.

## Fairway and Approach-Shot Strategy

For your fairway woods or your approach shot to the green, you should have a definite plan before you set up to hit the ball. While the fairway might look wide open and vast, some planning ahead can make your next shot easier. On all of your fairway and approach shots you should maintain the focus of a very specific target, no matter how open the shot may appear.

### Pick a Very Specific Target

You should do this for your fairway and approach shots. By selecting a small, specific target, your misses are more likely to remain playable. The fairway shot you hit right before your approach shot into the green should consider:

1. The angle you would like into the green for your approach shot.

2. The need to avoid "short siding" yourself.

3. Knowing your math so you can leave a comfortable distance into the flag.

This planning ahead will help you to produce easier, more successful approach shots to the green. Ideally, the angle you want to leave yourself to your target is one that does not require you to hit the ball up and over any unnecessary obstacle. If by aiming your fairway shot to the right edge of the fairway you can avoid having to go over the bunker on the left to get to the pin, you should do so.

You'll also want to avoid "short-siding" yourself. The definition of short-siding is to put your golf ball just off the side of the green to which the pin is closest. By doing this, you leave very little room for the ball to have time to roll, therefore requiring a more difficult approach shot. It would be better to leave ball so that your approach shot has plenty of green to work with and room for roll. Leaving the right angle to the pin and some room to work with between the edge of the green and the pin for your approach shot will allow you to choose a more user-friendly option.

If you know how far you hit each club and shot, and you know the distances at which you seem to have the most success, you can use a little minor math to leave yourself a favorable distance to your target for your approach shot. At Atlantic, on the back range we have small, circular sand greens at forty, sixty, eighty, and one hundred yards from the center of the tee for practice. The circle of sand is three feet in diameter. If you land the ball in the sand it immediately splashes and stops, so you definitely know when you have hit the target. I went to practice there as a result of a challenge from the head golf professional, Rick Hartmann, a terrific club professional and an accomplished player, who told me he had hit all four targets in twenty minutes. I wanted to see how long it would take me to hit all four, and while it took me longer than Rick, I was happy with my results. I also discovered that eighty yards was the most comfortable distance for me, so this would be a distance I might try to leave myself to my target, if I were unable to reach it in one shot or had the ability to get very close to the green.

Here is a situation:

160 yards to the green

Too far to reach in one shot

Love to hit thirty-yard bump and runs (a green skill)

The goal is to leave yourself thirty yards to the green, so you'll want to use a fairway wood that travels one hundred and thirty yards, and then hit your favorite bump and run.

Everyone has different favorite shots. Hopefully, when you did your initial testing in chapter 2 you were able to determine your strengths. These green-light shots are the ones you want to be setting up when you hit your fairway shot just before your approach shot into the green. For example, if you are a green-light chipper you will want to be sure to aim very carefully on the shot just before your approach shot, leaving yourself plenty of room for roll into the flag. This little bit of extra care can shave shots from your score by allowing you to use one of your stronger skills.

## Assess Risk Versus Reward for Better Decision Making

You've left yourself a less than ideal angle for your approach shot and there is a bunker between you and the flagstick. You now need to decide if there is enough potential reward in going over the bunker to take the risk. Risk should only be taken if there is probable reward, like shaving a stroke from your score. In this situation, you should ask yourself:

1. Is this a shot with which you are comfortable and having success?

2. Have you had success with this shot today or very recently?

3. If you do go up and over the bunker, is there enough room between the edge of the green and the pin to allow the ball to have enough time to realistically set down and get close?

If the answer to any or all of these questions is no, choose to avoid the unnecessary risk by playing around the bunker to the wider part of the green. You could play around the bunker, attempt to two-putt, and then just go to the next hole. If there is only minimal potential gain to your gamble, do not take it.

## *Aim and Align Carefully When Necessary*

When hitting your fairway shot to set up for your approach shot, remember that an exact landing area requires exact aim and alignment. I realize that aiming precisely may take a little more time and effort. An eye for detail can be very helpful here. It still amazes me how often I see golfers get completely set up to hit their shots without ever looking to the target even once. If you completely set up before you look to the target, you are much less likely to sufficiently correct any aiming or aligning problem. You should look to your target several times during your setup routine. Any-time you attempt to change a setup routine, it has to be a very conscious effort over time to make the new routine a habit, one you do without thinking. If you are not used to looking to your target while you are setting up, it will take some getting used to, but it is necessary and helps you aim exactly.

### To Aim Successfully Look to the Target

1. Look to the target.

2. Aim the club face to the target.

Be sure to look to your target several times during your setup routine.

3. Look to the target to double-check that the club face is correct.

4. Place your hands on the club.

5. Look to the target to see that the club face still looks correct.

6. Set your feet parallel to the target line.

7. Look to the target to double-check your visual perspective.

8. Go!

I think three to four times is an absolute minimum number for looking to the target for each setup routine. This should be true of all of your shots, including short-game shots and full swings.

## Play Away from Glaring Obstacles

Where are the places on your golf course where you absolutely do not want your golf ball to be? Is there a deep pot bunker from hell, or an area of particularly long rough that you absolutely cannot seem to get your club through? These are places you should try to avoid by playing strategically.

Keep the trouble spots in mind when you design your game plan. It may oftentimes be better for you to take a lesser club and play short or around these trouble spots, and then go over or around with a more manageable shot.

## *Putting Strategy*

As you become more proficient with your approach shots and your short-game shots you can strive to leave yourself makeable putts. These are a respectable distance away and preferably flat or slightly uphill. And I do realize that this strategy is many times easier said than done and requires a more advanced skill level. There also are times when it is better to leave yourself a little longer putt that is relatively flat, compared to a shorter putt on an "icy" downhill slope.

### Assess the Difficulty and Adjust Expectations Accordingly

You've done to the best of your ability on your approach to the green and now you have to assess your putt. Is it a manageable, user-friendly putt that you might possibly make, or at worst a two-putt, or is it a tricky putt, where you have be careful? If you fail to recognize the difficulty of some putts, you might not realize the care they require. The putts that require special attention are:

- **very downhill or uphill**

- **very undulating with a lot of curvature**

- **very long putts**

When you realize that a putt is difficult and understand that to two-putt would be an accomplishment, you are more likely to pay the necessary attention. For example, I have a fifteen-foot, severely downhill putt that is going to be very fast. On a flatter surface my goal might be different. I would be thinking about trying to put a nice stroke on the putt, aim the face very carefully, roll the ball the right speed, and hope that it goes in. But with a severe downhill slope my goal is completely different. I am respectful of the difficulty the slope adds, and while my goal is still to put a nice stroke on the ball, I will gently ease the ball down to the cup, hoping it settles very close. Even just short of the cup is absolutely fine. If the ball barely drops in the front edge of the cup, that is a nice bonus, but not my goal. I'm not trying to make the putt, but to roll it close enough to have a very simple tap in for my second putt. If you can recognize and respect the more difficult putts you are more likely to take the time necessary to prepare to roll a successful one.

## Learn Your Home-Course Greens

The more you play your home course, the more you should be able to read the greens and know how they roll. It is always helpful to learn from your mistakes. A putt that looks relatively benign can earn much more respect if, after several failures, you learn how to adjust for what you might not see with your eye. There are several greens at Atlantic Golf Club that I have trouble reading. But after playing the course enough, I have memorized how they roll and react and have been able to learn from my mistakes. It can be helpful to remember that each green will have a predominant tilt to help to aid in proper draining of the green in case of rain. By learning about this tilt you can often read the greens more efficiently.

### Most Greens Slope from the Back to the Front
This tendency of most golf greens can give you an idea of the predominant tilt, unless your eyes tell you otherwise. When the green is slightly tilted toward you it will be easier to see from the fairway as you approach. If you think about it, that makes sense. If the green slopes away from you so that the front is higher than the back, would you be able to see the putting surface as you approach? Probably not, and this is one way to help you to read the greens properly.

## Bunker Strategy: Get It Out, Get It On, or Get It Close

Your bunker strategy should match your skill level. How did you do in the bunker in your skills test?

### Get It Out!

If you struggle with your bunker play, you might want to lower your goals and expectations and just attempt to get the ball out of the sand. If this is the case, you should almost always aim to the shortest point to the grass. This may often require you to aim away from the pin, but it will help you to achieve your goal of getting out.

### Get It On!

Once you can get the ball consistently out of the sand, your next goal is to get the ball onto the green. This intermediate goal will require you to consider what obstacles you may wish to avoid in case you are in a little too short or long. You should look for an aiming line that will leave you with an acceptable next shot, should your distance control leave a little to be desired. It may be your best choice to aim away from the pin, if that would allow you to hit toward the larger part of the green, or if the ball accidentally went too far you would not be in another hazard, such as a bunker or water.

### Get It Close!

Once you can successfully get the ball out of the bunker and onto the green more times than not, your next goal is to get it close. This will require solid mechanics, good feel, and possibly more practice time. As you reach this stage of achieving distance control from the bunker, by varying the speed of your golf swing, you should be much more careful with your alignment of your club face to your target.

# Mental Tips

8

The right attitude can really help a lot at this point. I often laugh at the saying that golf is 90 percent mental, because I believe mechanics are much more important for most golfers, no matter how good their attitude. But as you look to lower your score, sending the right messages to your brain can certainly help.

## Oh Well!

Do you tend to get mad when you hit a bad shot? How long will you continue to be mad after a bad shot? Do you call yourself bad names? We all do. We all have. And while this is natural and normal, at some point you have to get past the anger and move on. After you express your anger, try saying to yourself, "Oh well." Actually try this. Say it out loud to yourself. The less you can overreact and move on to your next shot, the less you take the message internally, and the less it can affect your next shot.

You might want to try to be more like "Freddy." Have you ever watched Fred Couples play golf? He is a PGA Tour player who rarely reacts to a good/ bad shot either way. I often say to my student Victor, "You need to be more like Freddy," and he immediately knows what I mean.

If you can limit how negatively you react you are less likely to be noticed as not playing well. People are so self-absorbed with their own golf they will rarely notice your struggles, if you can be quiet about it. Now, I realize there is a point where enough is enough. If you continually hit the same poor shot over and over, "Oh well" is only going to work for so long. This is where the anger and frustration can be used to motivate you to take action to improve your skills through lessons and/or practice. Then it will be helpful in the long run.

## Don't Confuse Comfort with Correct

This is a saying I learned from Mike Adams, and it has really stuck with me. When you are working to improve your fundamentals and your skill level, it will be necessary for you to make changes. When you make a change, it is different by definition. In most cases, different will feel uncomfortable or awkward. In order to make necessary changes to improve, you must stick with the discomfort until the fundamental improves. In many cases, you can assume that if it feels bad, it is probably good. A grip change will very often fall into this category. When you place your hands on the grip in a different position, you will probably feel horribly uncomfortable. I am sympathetic to this in that I will only make a grip adjustment or change that will immediately improve the ball flight. If it feels uncomfortable every time you place your hands correctly on the grip and you move it back to its original incorrect position, you will never improve! If you stick with the uncomfortable change enough times and see that the ball flight is much better when the club face is more square at impact, you can move past the discomfort through the repeated proper holding of the club. It is much easier to stick with an uncomfortable change when you immediately see improvement.

## If You Are Thinking Something and It Works, Keep Thinking It

Have you ever played really well on your front nine, only to simply collapse on the back nine? We all have. In hindsight, what you were doing to be successful on the first half, you probably took for granted and failed to do on the second half. Whatever you consciously think when hitting successful golf shots should be continued. I almost always have self-talk when I play golf, and I have spoken with better players who have told me that they simply think of the target and not about their motion. But for the average golfer, I think the script that you provide yourself for each shot should be continually repeated until it no longer works. My father and I would often joke about this, because there is no guarantee that the thought that worked today, and seemed like "the answer" that we are all searching for forever, will work tomorrow. But it might work tomorrow, and you should continue until it does not work.

## Take Responsibility

If you hope to improve and lower your score you must take responsibility for your golf game, both the strengths and the weaknesses. No one can hit the shots for you, although sometimes that would be nice. An example is tending to top your fairway woods. If this is your most common mistake, why should you be surprised when it happens over and over again, if you have done nothing to improve the situation?

If you struggle with topping fairway woods, as many women do, you have to take responsibility and change something, or have a plan of attack when this happens. One of my students, Betty Sue, tends to top her fairway woods when she plays on the course, but not on the range, so during one of her playing lessons we devised a plan to handle this situation. We had her adjust her preparation and preshot routine, replacing a practice swing with a scrape drill. This kinesthetic drill of feeling the club head staying low to the ground past the golf ball, and sweeping the grass in a semicircle, helped her to transfer this feeling into her golf swing, producing much more solid, in-the-air, fairway shots. By having this game plan, she did not panic and was able to handle the situation when she did start to top her fairway woods. She was prepared for the situation and took responsibility for this weakness.

If you struggle with distance control on your long putts, why should it change if you don't take responsibility? This happened to me this past winter with my forehand in tennis. It was horrible. Not only was the form poor, but the results were embarrassing and I was getting very frustrated. So I took responsibility. I returned to my tennis professional, Brenda, for lessons. She had helped me before and thankfully she was able to help me again. The order we used to improve is the same one you can use.

## How to Improve

1. Identify the problem. First determine what mechanics are lacking and how to make the necessary changes. Understand how you are going to make the necessary change and feel free to ask as many questions as necessary to fully understand.

2. Consciously make the change. Once you've identified the problem, every time you hit a shot, think about what you are trying to do differently. It may be the setup, the motion, or both.

3. Understand the feedback from the ball. This is where practice will come into play. I know, I said it, the dreaded *P* word, but improvement requires experience and probably change, and change requires repetition with feedback. To make the improvement, you'll need to understand how to read the feedback you are given from the golf ball. Be sure also to go over this with your professional.

You must have someone you trust to help you with your golf. You've heard the saying, "Too many cooks spoil the soup." This is also true for golf. You need to find someone you trust to help you improve your golf. When you find the right person, it will be very obvious. A qualified teaching professional identifies the cause of the problem and explains it to you in terms that you can understand. This person is a safety net, someone you trust and feel comfortable with.

## Adjust Your Expectations to the Situation at Hand

Throughout your golf round and your golf experience you'll find yourself in a lot of different situations. You might play the same the golf course all of your life and still occasionally find yourself in a new place you've never been. Some of the places will be nice and user-friendly and others just flat-out difficult, or sometimes impossible. As situations increase in difficulty you must keep adjusting your expectations and your plan of attack. I often see the novice golfer lack respect for the difficulty of some golf shots.

The higher the degree of difficulty, the lower the quality of the potential results. Like gymnastics scores, the difficulty level of the routine determines the possible total score. In golf, the more difficult the shot, the more conservatively you should play.

### *"Should" Is Not a Good Golf Word*

I hear it used often, but it rarely is appropriate. In fact, the word generally does not work when applied to golf and is probably counterproductive.

"I should be better by now."

"I should be scoring lower."

"I should hit it farther."

"How far should I hit this club?"

There is no "should" in golf. What good are these statements doing for you? This might sound like tough love, but you might honestly believe you should be better and/or score lower, but you

Resistance training with a swing fan.

are not what we call a better player. So, if this applies to you, you have two choices: You can do something about it and take lessons and practice a lot, or you can make peace with the golf game that you do have.

You might also think you "should" hit the ball farther, or that with your 7 iron it "should" fly a certain distance. Nevertheless, it doesn't. You also have a choice here. You can work to increase your swing speed with resistance and speed training. Or you can make peace with how far you do hit the ball, lose the ego, and swing the club that will get you to your target, even if you do not hit your absolute bust-a-gut best.

I remember going through this phase when I was playing college golf as a freshman and sophomore. I would tend to underclub myself. My coach told me he always knew where my golf ball would be—just short of or on the front edge of the green. With

this understanding, a new set of graphite-shafted irons, and a little more experience, by my junior and senior years I hit the club I needed to get to my target and did not worry about what anyone else was using.

 ### Resistance and Speed Training

Learn to increase your swing speed and hit the ball farther requires both resistance and speed training. If you simply added resistance training, you might increase your strength but not necessarily your speed. It is necessary to have both. A swing fan is a wonderful method of resistance training. You should attempt to have the fan make as loud a swoosh at the bottom of your golf swing as possible.

Follow the fan swings by swooshing the grip end of your golf club. Turn any one of your golf clubs upside down and hold the club on the shaft just below the club head. Swing the shaft over

Speed training with an upside-down club.

your right shoulder. Make the grip swoosh at the bottom of your swing, and then swing the shaft over your left shoulder. The shaft of the club should tap it at your finish position. The higher the pitch and louder the swoosh, the more speed is generated. The more often you practice resistance and speed training, the more results you can expect.

I've seen this method of training produce incredible results for several of my students. If you do it once in a while it will help, but if you really want to see an improvement you must commit to using it over time. I watched one of my students, even to my amazement, increase her distance twenty yards per club within a half-hour lesson. Now she needs to repeat this process to retain the feel, but the improvement was so dramatic we were both surprised.

## Talk to Yourself Positively

Have you ever really paid attention to the way you talk to yourself or the messages you deliver during your round? Would you say: "Don't hit it in the bunker (the water, the rough, etc.)," or:

"I am going to take plenty of club, because it is better to be long than short," or:

"I always miss these short putts" right before you putt, or: "I am going to put the best possible stroke I know on this putt"?

When you play your next round of golf, listen to what you say to yourself. If the message is negative, try to turn it around and make it positive. If you are in the habit of negativity, as many golfers are, you cannot improve your self-talk until you are aware of the problem. Once you listen to yourself you might be surprised. It will take a commitment over time to change this pattern.

It is important to understand that your mind works in pictures. So, when you tell yourself not to hit your golf ball into the water your mind will see the water and disregard the "not." Use positive words and imagery. Retrain your negative instructions into positive ones, a good suggestion for life as well as golf.

# 9

# *How to Improve and Prepare for Your Golf Round*

**H**ow can you make your practice time more efficient and useful? What does it take be become a better golfer? What should you be doing right before you go to the first tee to be better prepared? Everyone is a little different. I have seen a lot of golfers improve dramatically, and they all got there in different ways. The challenge is finding a program that works for each individual. That will be your challenge: to find out what works for you. The following are merely suggestions to expand and develop once you see what produces the best results for you. Your personality will almost always play a large part of what it takes for you to improve.

Whatever practice time you do have needs to be useful; therefore, you should have a goal or a specific purpose. It might be to make a mechanical change, for example, improving your left-hand grip position, or it might be results-oriented like making sure the bottom of your club hits the ground every time to minimize your topping problem. Realize that improvement takes time and commitment. True, improvement is a process and not the "answer" that so many golfers seem to be endlessly seeking. Think of the things in your life that you are good at doing, and of the things that are important to you. Did they come overnight? Or did you have to work for them? I would guess they took work, time, and commitment. I still work hard every day at trying to be a better golf instructor, whether it is an effort to communicate more clearly, or to increase my technical knowledge. I have been very fortunate to be able to observe other wonderful instructors teach, and I have learned something from all of them. I feel very lucky and thank those who have shared their knowledge.

You might want to have specific practice drills to help to make these improvements. If you have been assigned a practice drill by your professional, it is very important that you do this homework. It might be as simple as taking practice swings to learn how to consistently sweep the grass. Improvement is usually easier when seen over time, rather than day to day or week to week. Are you better than you were three years ago? Are you better than you were two years ago? Are you better than you were one year ago? I hope for you that you can answer yes to these questions. If you answer to all three is no, then it is time to assess why. If you are not getting better, other than being physically challenged and just trying to maintain your level of success, you have to take some responsibility and make some changes to your current regimen.

## Analyze Your Previous Round and Work on Your Weaknesses

Your practice time should take into consideration your patterns on the golf course. Your round analysis can be as specific or general as you wish. You could keep track of:

1. the number of putts

2. the percentages of up and downs

3. fairway hits

4. the greens in regulation—you might need to consider your personal par for higher handicappers

5. the penalty shots

Or you can mark small notes on your scorecard to help to remind you of specific difficulties throughout your round. I usually think this is a little easier and more realistic, as far as keeping statistics, unless you are trying to play golf for a living, and then I think you need to keep more accurate statistics. These small notes should quickly identify where you are having trouble during your round. Whatever areas of your game are lacking during your round should be ones focused on during your practice time.

Keep small notes during your round to identify what you need to practice.

## The Magic Ten Minutes

You do not necessarily need a lot of practice time to improve. As a result of your analysis of previous rounds, try picking the area of your game that is most lacking and practice that one basic skill for ten minutes: ten whole minutes on one particular shot. It does not sound like a long time, but how often do you spend ten minutes hitting three-foot putts, or ten minutes on really long putts, or ten minutes on your thirty-yard pitch shot? The beginning part of your ten minutes will probably consist of checking your mechanics and seeing that you are able to hit the shot. Beyond the mechanical check you will at some point transition into developing your feel for distance control. If after this ten minutes you see a noticeable improvement, it might be a good idea to try this ten minutes again later.

### Set Specific Goals over Time and Have a Plan

It takes time to turn a weakness into a strength. What is the weakest part of your game? The skills tests you took in chapter 2 help you to identify this. Take this weakest skill and set a goal over time to improve. An example would be to be a better chipper in four months. My plan to improve the skill over the next four months includes spending ten minutes twice a week hitting a very generic chip and practicing my setup station. I will want to check my process within this four-month period. After two months ask yourself, "Am I getting better?" If I am, I will continue with my practice schedule. If not, I might want to increase my time assigned to practice.

Also consider asking your golf professional for a more specific practice schedule. I have started to design these, including what to do and the number of repetitions. I always try to be realistic about the time required because I realize that life can get in the way, limiting practice time for golf. It does not necessarily take a lot of time, but it does take focused time.

Part of having focused practice time can include using a setup station for each area of your game. This is used to make sure that you are practicing properly and help you easily identify any mistakes.

## Setup Stations for Quality Practice

### Putting

Set one club just outside of your golf ball so that an extension of the shaft points to the right edge of the cup. The line parallel to it down the middle of the golf ball should point directly to the center of the cup. This will help you check your putter face alignment, body alignments, and the path of your stroke. Your putter face should be perpendicular to this golf club and the line through your shoulders should be parallel to this club on the ground. I also like to see the other body lines be parallel to this club, including hips, feet and eyes, but that is a preference. You can also check that the path of your stroke runs parallel to the setup club and with a slight semicircular shape to your longer putting strokes. Your putter should not cross the shaft of the club.

Setup station for chipping.

### Chipping

My setup station for chipping will include two golf clubs, one for alignment and the other for ball position. Set one club just next to your golf ball, pointing slightly to the right of your target so that a parallel line over the top of the ball would point directly to the target. Use this club to help check your club face alignment, your aim, and the path of your chipping stroke. Your club face should be perpendicular and your shoulders parallel to the club on the ground. Your stance might be slightly open, with your left foot slightly farther from this club than your right. You can also use this club to check the path of your stroke because it should run relatively parallel to this club.

Your setup station for pitching and your full swing will be the same.

Place a second club perpendicular to the alignment club between your feet to check your ball position. Be sure to line the ball up with the extension of this shaft and to leave enough room between these clubs to ensure that you will not be hitting them during your stroke. If you choose to center your ball position for chipping, the club shaft should line up with the center of your heels. If you choose to position your ball farther back in your stance, the club shaft should line up with the inside of your right foot. Be careful to always position the club heads back behind the golf ball for safety reasons.

You can choose to add a third club six to eight inches behind your golf ball to ensure crisper contact. This is produced by the more descending angle of attack in chipping, as a result of your weight being left. This club will help you check that you maintain your weight favoring your left foot. If your weight stays properly left, your club head should easily clear this club shaft on your chipping stroke, but if you incorrectly shift your weight back to your right foot and try to "scoop" or "lift" your golf ball by swinging low to high, you can incorrectly contact this club. Be sure that you are only practicing small chips, as I would not want you to damage your club or yourself.

## Pitching

My setup station for pitching includes two clubs. One is for alignment and the other for ball position as well as shaft angle.

Set one club just outside the golf ball parallel to your target line and point it slightly to the right of the target. This club is used to help you aim your club face and align your body. Your club face should be perpendicular and your body lines, including feet, hips, shoulders, and eyes, should be parallel to this club.

Place a club between your feet and perpendicular to the alignment club. This club will be used for ball position and shaft angle. Your heels should be equidistant from the club to help you double-check that your ball position is centered and the shaft of your sand wedge matches the club on the ground, and that the end of your club points toward your belly button. By using this club between your feet you can check whether the shaft angle of your sand wedge is correct as this would allow you to use the bounce properly. The shaft should not lean forward or back for pitching, but stand straight up and down pointing toward your belly button.

## Full Swing

Your setup station for a full swing is much like that for pitching, in that it includes two clubs, one for aim and alignment and the other for ball position. As in your setup station for pitching, set one club just next to your golf ball, parallel to your target line and pointing slightly to the right of your target, with the club head behind your golf ball and turned out for safety. This club will help you to check that your club head is perpendicular and that your body lines are parallel. In that way it is helping you learn to aim and align precisely.

The second club is set perpendicular to this club to help you to check your ball position. For safety, be sure to leave yourself enough room between the two clubs so there is no chance that you will contact either on your swing. Your feet will relate to this club, depending upon your club of choice.

Irons: heels equidistant

Fairway woods: left heel slightly closer to the shaft than the right heel

Woods from a tee: shaft in line with the inside of the left heel

Setup stations help your practice time be more productive. Rather than wasting your time practicing incorrectly, you can insure that you are setting up properly, making it much easier to produce the desired results.

## Knowing Your Game

To lower your golf score it is important to know your own golf game. An example is the ability to know your tendencies and read the feedback from your missed shots. A small notebook that you keep in your golf bag can be very helpful. Each time you discover what causes a specific problem you can write it down, giving yourself a personal log and probably a pretty educated plan of attack for the future. Home visiting my family, I found the old notebooks from when I was playing professionally, and it was amazing how the fundamentals I was working on then are still the same ones I am aware of now. We all tend to repeat the same mistakes. This notebook helps cut the frustration time.

Do you know what causes you to top your golf ball? If it never gets into the air at all, you have contacted the ball above its equator. Your first step in understanding your mistakes is knowing how the club has incorrectly contacted the ball. When you top the ball it could be that you are standing too far away, or that your posture is not correctly bent forward from your hips, causing you to be off balance. Learn how to read what the golf ball tells you.

Does your ball tend to curve one way more than the other? What causes this? If you do not know, you need to find a professional who can identify the cause for you. It could be your grip, alignment, or swing. You have to educate yourself to be able to correct and this takes time because there are so many opposites in golf. An example is tending to aim too far to the right, which can cause your golf ball to hook to the left and vise versa. Learn what your tendencies are and how to correct them.

Another facet or managing your game is knowing your math. Do you know how far you hit each of your clubs? You should! There is no excuse for not knowing. If you do not, attach a small yardage chart to your golf bag and start making decisions for yourself. Do you know what short-game shot to use and when? If you didn't before, you should now. If not, attach a small copy of a short-game cheat sheet to your golf bag. This will help you to make your own decisions. While this might leave your prince charming with nothing to do but worry about his golf game, it will help you be more confident about making decisions for yourself. And so what if you make a mistake? Make the decision, and if it is the wrong one, learn from it and make a better decision next time.

Attach your own yardage chart to your golf bag to be more self-sufficient.

## Basic Knowledge

To make it possible to execute consistent golf shots, you must have a basic knowledge of how to handle the different situations you come across on the golf course every day. When I teach, I think it is important that my students understand what they should do in these situations and why. If you understand why you set up as you do for a bunker shot, for example, I think it is much easier to remember the next time, when I am not there with the safety net right underneath them. I know I drive some students a little crazy with the fact that I will have them explain to me what they should do in various situations, so that I am confident that when they are kicked out of the nest they will fly.

The proper concept for each situation is important and while the level of your execution will vary, your odds are much better if you feel confident that what you are trying to do is technically correct.

A great example of this is uneven lies. Do you know how to adjust to a side-hill lie with the ball above your feet? You must if you hope to be successful. Do not feel bad if you do not know how to handle all of these situations. It takes time and experience. Golf is a never-ending quest for how to manage your own golf game. You would be amazed how many good players cannot define what they do for different situations, but they often adjust naturally through instinct and experience. I have seen several tour players who did not understand what they were trying to do and actually perceived the opposite of what was truly occurring. The good news for them is they are very successful and have adjusted out of instinct.

The adjustments you make will not only apply to your full swing on an uneven lie, but for all of your short-game shots including the sand. If you do not know how to adjust, your odds for a successful result plummet. Many of my students have a difficult time remembering how to handle uneven lies, so a small chart is included on page 221 in the Appendix. You can attach to your golf bag along with your yardage chart and your simplified short-game cheat sheet.

## Your Warm-Up

What do you do right before your round to warm yourself up? How can you get the most out of whatever time you have? What you do right before you play has a great effect on your score. Here are specific goals for your warm up. This is not the time to experiment or try a new swing. Your skill level is not going to drastically improve during your warm-up, you can only play to the level that you have earned to this point. You have to dance with who you take to the dance.

One of my very favorite students, Julie, talked me into running in a half-marathon, even though I was not a runner. She sent me the application as well as a couple of books on running. I read the books and did exactly what the one that I preferred told me to do to prepare. On the morning of the race, at 4:30 A.M. in Disney World, in a corral with 22,000 other runners, a woman next to me said, "I wish I had trained a little more." I remember feeling this great sense of confidence and accomplishment because I had prepared and was ready. Julie had given me the tools and I thank her very much for that, but I had done the work and preparation. Marathons are much like golf; you must prepare and you must play the game that you have. I would not have been able to run a full marathon that day, because I had not prepared for it. So play the game you have and if you hope to improve, prepare.

Here are the goals of your preround warm up:

1. **Loosen up: Whether you stretch, practice swing, or hit golf balls, you'll want to physically warm up your body to avoid injury.**

2. **Assess ball flight: What is your golf ball doing today? How is your swing working? The golf balls you hit prior to your round will give you some insight. This is an important determination because it will tell you the adjustments you need to make in your game plan. If your ball is curving right during your warm-up, compensate during your round by aiming left, enough to accommodate the curvature until proven otherwise. If you are tending to top the ball, aim around the obstacles that require airtime until proven otherwise.**

   I've gotten much better at this assessment over time. By not trying to hit shots that are over my head and playing smarter, relying on my short game, I have made fewer big numbers during my rounds of golf.

3. **Warm up your short game:** Be sure to hit several pitch and chip shots making sure that the differences are clear in your head. This will give you an idea of the level of success for each shot.

4. **Please roll some medium-to-longer putts:** I add the word "please" because it is so important you roll a few longer putts to get a feel for your stroke as well as the speed of the greens on a particular day. Many golfers do not do this, even though it is so important. I do not want any excuses for not knowing the speed of the first green.

Once you have completed your warm-up be sure you are prepared with the necessary tools, Be sure to have plenty of golf balls, tees, and a marker or two to mark your golf ball on the green. Then get to the first tee on time without feeling rushed. By being prepared in advance you can avoid arriving in a panic, feeling unprepared. When you feel calm and prepared, these feelings carry over into your golf game and help to lower your score.

# Playing a Round of Golf:
# Nine Holes

**10**

**W**hen designing your personal game plan, take into consideration your strengths (green skills), the shots you will use most often, as well as your weaknesses (red skills), the shots you will use only when you have exhausted all other options. Consider listing your skills on a sheet of paper under the appropriate color so that you have them more clearly defined in your head. An example:

- **Green skills: short putts, long putts, short irons**

- **Yellow skills: chipping, fairway woods, tee shots, distance**

- **Red skills: pitching, long irons, sand**

Listing your skills and having the list right in front of you can help you make better decisions, choosing skills that have a higher chance for success. You also adjust your game plan throughout your round, based upon your results and the feedback from your golf ball. Part of this adjusting includes not using a skill that seems to be failing you on a particular day. For example, if you are normally a green-skill fairway wood player and today your usual choices aren't working, do not use them and try using a longer iron in their place.

This golfer's model for playing a nine-hole round is designed with my average female student in mind. Feel free to adjust your game plan to your particular strengths and weaknesses. The model will show you how to manage your golf game by adjusting throughout the round and managing the golf course with the least risk while focusing on your most successful abilities. I'll share with you the thought process that I went through while playing a round, how I handled various situations, and the planning that was involved throughout the nine-hole round. If the thought process I went through is different from your own, you might find it helpful to read this section several times.

## The Warm-Up

I started with a few half-swings with my sand wedge (a pitch shot) and they were fine, other than the couple that did not quite hit the ground. They never got into the air and rolled a lot.

I then hit the even-numbered irons, the pitching wedge, 8 iron, and the 6 iron, and the shots were all pretty good. I hit the odd irons to warm up yesterday. Next, I warmed up my fairway woods. The 9 wood and the 7 wood were good. The 5 wood was OK, but not as consistent as the others. Then I hit some tee shots with both my 3 wood and my driver. They were both fine, but curving slightly to the right. Finally, I rolled a handful of medium-to-longer putts to check my stroke and get a feel for the greens. They seemed a little quicker than normal, but my stroke felt good.

## My Yardage Chart: Measure in Yards

Sand wedge: 40–50

Pitching wedge: 60–70

9 iron: 70–80

8 iron: 75–85

7 iron: 80–90

6 iron: 90–100

5 iron: 95–105

4 iron: 100–110

9 wood: 110–120

7 wood: 120–130

5 wood: 130–140

3 wood: 140–150

1 wood (driver): 150–160

## *The Round*

To the first tee:

### Hole #1

   Par 4 • 320 yards • Personal par 5 (3 shots + 2 putts)

**Tee shot:** I used my 3 wood to tee off with because was just getting started and it seemed to be a little more consistent. There was a fairway bunker just off the right side of the fairway, so because some of my warm-up tee shots were curving to the right, I placed my tee into the right side of the tee box and aimed for the left side of the fairway.

*Results:* I hit a respectable tee ball that started down the left side of the fairway and curved back nicely to the center of the fairway, traveling 140 yards. That left 180 yards to the center of the green.

**Fairway shot:** For my first fairway wood I used my 7 wood. I am a little more consistent with my 7 wood and wanted to help my confidence early in the round. I was going to aim to the right center of the fairway. There is a bunker on the left side of the green that I did not want to have to hit the ball over on my approach shot, because the pin is on the left side of the green.

*Results:* The 7 wood was OK, but not great, traveling 100 yards. The ball got up into the air, but not as much as it could have, because my club did not quite sweep the grass enough. But even though I did not hit it perfectly, it was just fine and in the right side of the fairway, setting me up well for my approach to the pin on a left side of the green. This left 80 yards remaining to the center of the green.

**Approach shot:** I had 80 yards left to the center of the green, but the pin was located in the back, so I added 5 more yards for a total of 85 yards. My yardage chart attached to my golf bag

**Hole 1**

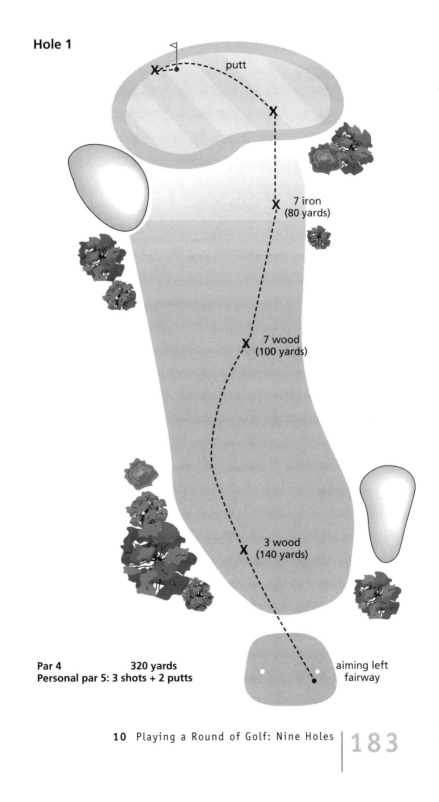

putt

7 iron
(80 yards)

7 wood
(100 yards)

3 wood
(140 yards)

aiming left
fairway

Par 4            320 yards
Personal par 5: 3 shots + 2 putts

reminded me that my 7 iron travels between 80 and 90 yards, so it was perfect here. I aimed a little right of the flag to avoid the left bunker and to aim to the wider side of the green.

*Results:* The 7 iron was fine. The ball traveled 80 yards and was on the front right side of the green. I left myself a longer putt (green skill) and avoided any risk of the sand (red skill).

**Putt:** I had a longer putt that was slightly uphill, in addition, the green tilts from the right to the left, so I aimed a little right of the cup. It was a longer putt, and I was more concerned with rolling the ball the right distance. Because I hit some warm-up putts, I was feeling relatively confident. I took my practice strokes, looking at the target and keeping in mind that it was uphill, but also remembering from my warm-up that the greens were a little faster than normal that day. I then aimed the line of my putter face slightly to the right of the hole, set my feet parallel, and made my stroke as much like my practice stroke as possible.

*Results:* My putt was just a little too firm. It rolled four feet past the hole and curved left as it went by the cup.

**Four-foot putt:** Since I closely watched my putt curve left when it passed by the cup, I knew what followed the same path and curved right when I stroked it from the other side of the cup. I was very careful to aim the wording on the ball to the left edge of the cup, and after my practice strokes, careful to match the line on the putter to the wording on the ball, as well as carefully set the line through my toes parallel to this line. I took one last look to the left side of the cup, reminded myself to keep my lower body very still, and made the stroke.

*Results:* Good news! Right in the center of the cup.

## Hole #2

**Par 3 • 140 yards • Personal par 4 (2 shots + 2 putts)**

**Tee shot:** I will tee off with my 3 wood because it was the right club for the distance. This was also confirmed by my tee shot on the first hole. There was a bunker blocking the right side of the green and the pin was tucked just over the sand. I teed my ball on the left side of the teeing ground because it did not require me to have to go over the sand to get to the green. I aimed to the very left side of the green to avoid the sand and also to play for my natural left-to-right ball flight that was also confirmed by my tee shot on the first hole.

*Results:* I hit the 3 wood very well, but it did not curve right, so it ended up just left of the green and pin-high. I was perfectly happy because I avoided the sand (red skill) and set myself up to be able to chip (green skill).

**Approach shot:** I was in my short game because I was less the distance to the pin than my sand wedge travels with full swing. I had a good lie. I needed more roll than carry and I was within five steps from the edge of the green, so I chipped. I needed twice the amount of roll compared to the carry, so I used my pitching wedge that travels ⅓ carry and ⅔ roll. I remembered to grip down, step in closer, narrow my stance and lean left. Once I set up I took my practice stroke, just like my putting stroke, looking where I wanted the ball to land while sweeping the grass. I then set up to the golf ball, being very careful to aim the club face to my target, then adjusted my distance from the golf ball by stepping my feet. I then tried to repeat what I felt in my practice stroke, this time with the ball in the way.

# Hole 2

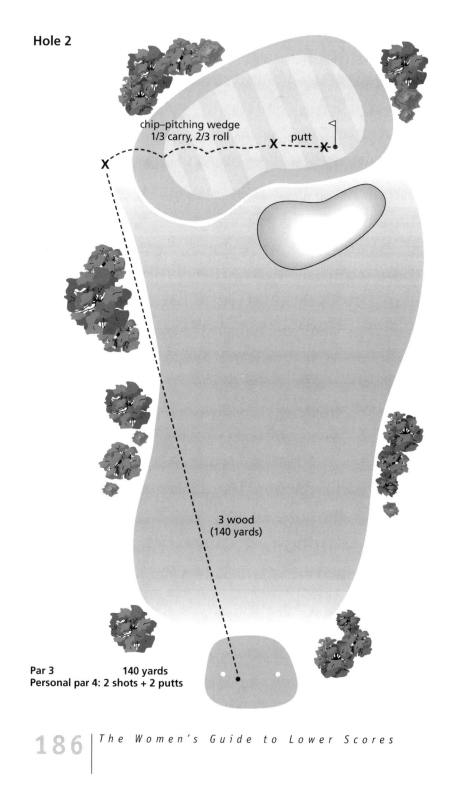

chip–pitching wedge
1/3 carry, 2/3 roll

putt

3 wood
(140 yards)

Par 3          140 yards
Personal par 4: 2 shots + 2 putts

*Results:* I hit a good chip that was a little too soft, so I left myself a ten-foot putt.

**Putt:** My ten-foot putt was a little uphill, so I aimed a little past the cup. I aimed at the wording on the ball to point to the cup because I thought it was a straight putt, and after my practice stroke I was careful to match the putter face and my feet to the line on the ball. Once I set up, I repeated my practice stroke with the ball in the way and held the finish. My goal here was to roll the ball at the right speed and to get it close.

*Results:* I rolled the ball within ten inches of the cup and putted out from there because I was not standing in anyone's line to do so.

### Hole #3

Par 5 • 490 yards • Water crosses the fairway 100 yards from the green with a pond on the right side of the green. • Personal par 6 (4 shots + 2 putts)

**Tee shot:** There was no trouble to be aware of from the tee, and both of my tee shots on the number one and two were good, so I was feeling confident and graduated to my driver. My 3 wood curved slightly to the right on number one, so I also planned for this on the driver by placing my tee into the ground on the right side of the tee box and aiming to the left side of the fairway. I took an extra practice swing to have time to adjust for the longer club.

*Results:* My tee shot with my driver was OK, but not great. It ended up in the fairway, but because I missed it, it did not travel as far as my 3 wood, traveling only 130 yards, leaving 360 yards to the green.

**Fairway wood:** I still had a long way to the green and did not need to be concerned with the water hazard, because it was still far away. I had a side-hill lie with the ball above my feet, so I needed to grip lower on whatever club I chose, because the ball was physically closer to me than on a flat lie. I aimed a little more to the right to compensate for the ball's tending to curve left from this lie. I remembered this because the ball tends to do what the hill does. Since the hill leaned left, that was the direction that the ball would tend to curve. I also remembered never to aim where a straight shot would get me into trouble. I chose to use my 7 wood from the fairway, again because I have the most confidence in this club, especially on the uneven lie.

## Hole 3

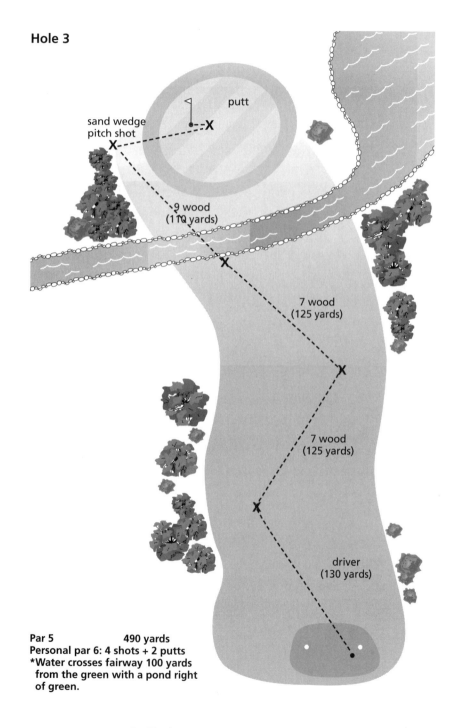

putt

sand wedge
pitch shot

9 wood
(110 yards)

7 wood
(125 yards)

7 wood
(125 yards)

driver
(130 yards)

**Par 5         490 yards**
**Personal par 6: 4 shots + 2 putts**
***Water crosses fairway 100 yards**
**from the green with a pond right**
**of green.**

*Results:* I hit my 7 wood well, but it stayed straight rather than curving slightly left, and the ball landed on the right side of the fairway. It traveled 125 yards, so I had 235 yards remaining to the center of the green.

**Fairway wood:** The 235 yards remaining to the green left me 135 yards to the water hazard that ran across the fairway 100 yards from the green. My 7 wood traveled 125 yards on the last shot, so I stuck with it. I aimed to the left side of the fairway to play away from the water on the right side down by the green.

*Results:* I hit another good 7 wood, traveling 125 yards, left-center fairway, which left 110 yards to the center of the green. I was gaining confidence in my fairway woods.

**Approach shot:** I had 110 yards to the green center where the flag was located. Since there was water on the right side of the green, I aimed to the far left side of the green. 110 yards is between a 4 iron and a 9 wood, and since I had a lot of confidence in my fairway woods that day I used the 9 wood.

*Results:* I hit the 9 wood well but aimed a little too far left, pin high and about 15 yards left of the green.

**Short-game shot:** I had 25 yards to the pin, so I was in my short game. I had a good lie so all options were available to me. I had approximately 15 steps of longer grass to carry and about 10 steps of green to work with, so I needed more carry than roll. This meant I had to pitch the golf ball. I decided to pitch, so I used my sand wedge and positioned my golf ball in the center of my stance, with the end of the club pointing to my belly button, so that the bottom of the club rested properly on its bounce. I attempted to carry the ball 20 yards, keeping in mind that it is better to be long than short, to insure that the ball carries the longer grass. Twenty yards is about half-swing for my sand wedge, so I lowered my hands on the grip to halfway and narrowed my stance to half width. When I took my practice swings I was sure to hear the bottom of the club "thump" the ground.

*Results:* I hit a good pitch shot that rolled just past the pin. I was happy with this result because I know it is better to be long than short. I had a 15-foot downhill putt remaining.

**Putt:** Because the putt was downhill I tried to roll the ball close rather than be aggressive and risk rolling too far.

*Results:* I rolled the putt at the right speed to about 15 inches from the cup and was careful to aim the face on the short putt to tap in.

## Hole #4

**Par four • 300 yards • Long grassy area necessary to clear on tee shot • Personal par 5 (3 shots + 2 putts)**

**Tee shot:** I used my 3 wood to tee off to ensure clearing the long grass. I placed my tee on the right side of the tee box to play for my left-to-right ball flight by aiming into the left side of the fairway.

*Results:* I hit a good tee shot that stayed straight and traveled 140 yards into the left side of the fairway. I had 160 yards left to the green.

**Fairway wood:** I was feeling very confident with my fairway woods, so I graduated from my 7 wood to my 5 wood and aimed to the right side of the fairway. This helped me to avoid the bunker guarding the left side of the green and left a clear approach shot to the pin, one where I did not need to go over either bunker. My best 5 wood only travels 140 yards maximum, a guarantee that my ball would stop short of both bunkers.

*Results:* I hit my 5 wood very well but a little too far right. My ball ended up in the rough 20 yards short and right of the green, with a clear approach angle to the pin.

**Short-game approach:** I was in my short game because I was only 20 yards to my target. My golf ball was sitting down deep in the grass, so I needed to adjust my setup by moving my ball position more in line with the instep of my right foot to help me to contact the ball before the grass, to drop my left foot back slightly, realigning my shoulders parallel to the target line, and to lean my weight onto my left foot. Leaning left produces a steeper

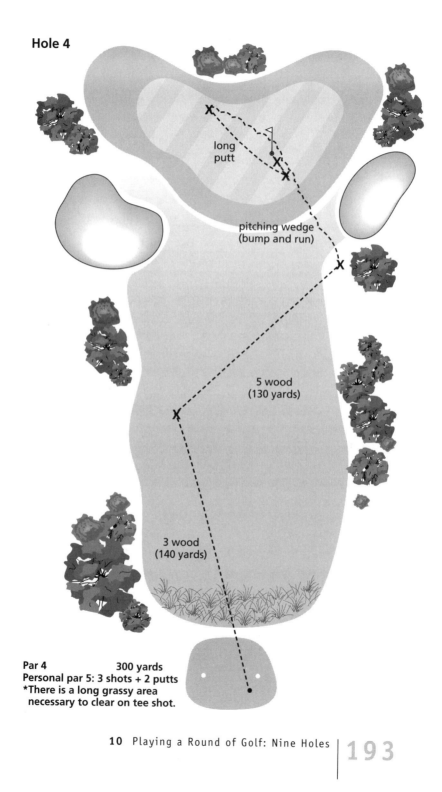

Hole 4

long
putt

pitching wedge
(bump and run)

5 wood
(130 yards)

3 wood
(140 yards)

Par 4          300 yards
Personal par 5: 3 shots + 2 putts
*There is a long grassy area
  necessary to clear on tee shot.

angle of attack and helps to extract a ball from long grass. Because these setup changes were necessary to get the ball out of the long rough, I needed to plan for more roll and land the ball short of the green, giving me room to then roll onto the putting surface. Normally I would use my 9 iron for this distance bump and run, but because the ball would roll more due to my setup, I used my pitching wedge instead.

*Results:* I hit the bump and run quite well, but because I was sure to accelerate through the forward stroke, the ball came out more cleanly than I had planned, and it rolled to the back of the green, leaving quite a long putt.

**Putt:** I had a long putt that was downhill and curving from right to left. I was sure to take my practice strokes looking slightly to the right and short of the cup to compensate for the downhill. I then carefully aimed my putter face and my body and reminded myself to be sure to keep my lower body very steady and repeat the same size stroke I felt in my practice.

*Results:* I took a little larger stroke than necessary and the ball rolled approximately ten feet past the cup.

**Ten-foot putt:** While returning from the other side of the cup I watched my golf ball curve left and roll by the cup, so I knew it would curve right on the return uphill trip. I carefully aimed my putter face and attempted to roll ball at the right speed.

*Results:* I made a nice stroke but the ball came up slightly short, so I tapped in for my three-putt. While I was not excited about three-putting, I realized my mistake was hitting my bump and run too far, leaving myself a more difficult first putt and that I did not roll the ball closer to the hole.

## Hole #5

Par 3 • 135 yards • Two bunkers guarding entrance to the putting green • Personal par 4 (2 shots + 2 putts)

**Tee shot:** Because there were two large bunkers at the entrance to the green, I teed off with a club that would land the ball short of both bunkers. If I used my 3 wood to carry the bunkers, even if I hit it perfectly, the shot probably would not be high enough and the ball would remain on the green. Therefore there was not enough reward for taking this risk. Instead, I teed off with my 9 wood and played for short of the green. I also was very careful with my aiming and aligning to leave myself a good angle to the pin, located in the center back, that would allow me to hit a bump and run.

*Results:* The 9 wood was fine, and because I was very careful to pick an intermediate target to aim over, I left myself with an open approach angle to the flag and did not have to go over either bunker.

**Short-game approach:** I was in my short game because I only had thirty yards left to the pin. The fairway grass was cut very short, so I did not have any ground to carry and I was more than five steps from the edge of the green, so I hit a bump and run. At thirty yards, hitting a bump and run, I used my 8 iron. I remembered to lean left throughout this stroke to help me hit the ground and assist with good solid contact.

*Results:* I stroked my bump and run very well and hit it quite solidly. The ball rolled to just short of the pin and was ten feet away.

**Hole 5**

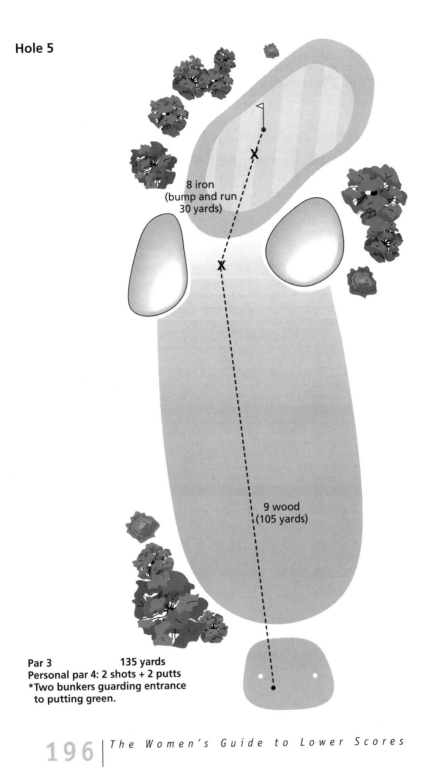

8 iron
(bump and run
30 yards)

9 wood
(105 yards)

Par 3             135 yards
Personal par 4: 2 shots + 2 putts
*Two bunkers guarding entrance
  to putting green.

**Ten-foot putt:** Because I played the hole intelligently, I had a putt to possibly make a three on the hole, which was one better than my personal par. The putt was straight and slightly uphill. I was careful about aiming the wording on the ball and my putter face, my body alignments, and rolling the ball at the right speed.

*Results:* Because I concentrated very hard on keeping my lower body still I was very happy to have made a 3 on the hole.

## Hole #6

Par 4 • 280 yards • Slight dogleg to the left with fairway bunkers surrounding the approach fifty yards from the green and closer. • Personal par 5 (3 shots + 2 putts)

**Tee shot:** I teed off with my 3 wood from the right side of the tee box and aimed to left center of the fairway. There was no need to attempt to hit my driver here. I was taking an unnecessary risk with little reward because the approach area was so severely guarded by the fairway bunkers.

*Results:* I did not hit my 3 wood particularly well, but it ended up traveling straight into the fairway, traveling 130 yards but very low. I would pay special attention on my next tee shot to try to clip the tee out of the ground, avoiding the very low ball flight.

**Fairway shot:** Because the approach to the green was guarded by so many fairway bunkers, I attempted to hit an iron that would stay short of them. My goal was to leave my golf ball just short of the farthest bunker from the green. Since I hit my tee shot 130 yards and wanted to leave myself 50 yards to the green, I needed to hit my fairway shot 100 yards, which according to my yardage chart was my 5 iron. My golf ball was on a side-hill lie with the ball below my feet. Because of this, I stepped in slightly closer toward my golf ball. Because the ball was physically farther from me than in a flat lie, I aimed slightly left because the ball tended to curve to the right from this lie. Balls tend to curve the way the hill slopes, and since the hill sloped to the right relative to the target, I knew that my golf ball would tend to curve that way.

**Hole 6**

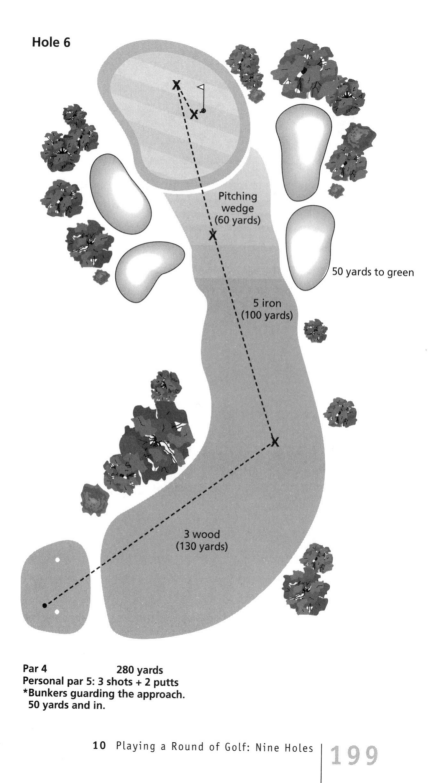

Pitching
wedge
(60 yards)

50 yards to green

5 iron
(100 yards)

3 wood
(130 yards)

Par 4          280 yards
Personal par 5: 3 shots + 2 putts
*Bunkers guarding the approach.
 50 yards and in.

*Results:* My 5 iron traveled straight but low into the left side of the fairway, leaving it 55 yards to the pin that was located in the right center of the green.

**Approach shot:** I was happy with the angle I had left myself, because I did not have to go over any of the bunkers. When I consulted my yardage chart, I saw that my sand wedge, which travels a maximum of 50 yards, would not be quite enough. But my pitching wedge in a full swing traveled a minimum of 60 yards, so I needed to take slightly less than a full swing with this club. To help me to reduce the swing I gripped down on the handle and narrowed my stance a small amount. When I took my practice swing I was sure to keep in mind that I wanted slightly less than a full swing and the bottom of the club to brush the grass.

Note: It is very common to have a gap in yardage between the sand wedge and the pitching wedge. The golf club manufacturers decreased the loft in the pitching wedge to help the ball travel farther, while leaving the loft of the sand wedge the same. Those smart marketing people were able to sell you a new set of clubs because your golf ball appeared to travel farther, and also sell you another club because now you needed a club that traveled a distance between your sand wedge and your newly improved pitching wedge that is actually a 9 iron in loft. If there is too large a gap between your sand wedge and your pitching wedge, you might consider adding a gap wedge, sometimes called a utility or a *A* wedge. Manufacturers often use different names for this wedge, just to add to our confusion.

The new pattern in women's golf clubs is to replace the longer irons with a hybrid club that is a cross between an iron and a wood. I think this is a great idea, but may take a little time to perfect.

*Results:* My three-quarter pitching wedge ended up being more like my full swing and traveled to the back of green, leaving a thirty-foot, left-to-right, downhill putt.

**Thirty-foot putt:** Because my putt was downhill and curving from left to right, my intended target was a spot short and left of the cup. When I took my practice strokes this was the spot where I focused. My goal was to roll ball the right speed and get it close enough to the hole to be able to tap it in. I was careful to aim at my putter face, aligning my body to my imaginary cup that was short and left of the actual cup.

*Results:* I rolled the ball the right speed but played a little bit too much break, so I left myself three feet from the cup on the left.

**Three-foot putt:** I had a slightly downhill three-foot putt that could curve slightly left to right. When I aimed the wording on the ball I pointed it slightly left center of the cup but was careful not to play for too much break. In a putt of this length I generally do not want to aim outside of the cup. Once I set myself up I remembered to keep my lower body still and to wait until I heard the ball go into the cup before I turned my head to look.

*Results:* The ball fell into the left center of the cup, confirming that on a putt this short it is better not to aim outside of the hole.

## Hole #7

Par 5 • Several fairway bunkers on the right side of the fairway affecting the tee shot • 450 yards • Personal par 6 (4 shots + 2 putts)

**Tee shot:** Because there were three large fairway bunkers just off to the right side of the fairway for the tee shot, I teed off with my 3 wood teeing the ball slightly higher. I also made sure that my practice swing hit the ground, a correction of my previous tee shot that traveled a little bit too low. I placed my tee into the ground on the right side of the tee box because this was the side of my trouble, and aimed into the left center fairway.

*Results:* My 3 wood was better this time. I was successful in clipping the tee and seeing the ball travel higher than at the previous hole. My ball traveled 135 yards and, because it was a par 5, I still had a long way to go to the green.

**Fairway wood:** Because I was on a slight downhill lie, where my left foot was slightly lower than my right, I needed to have my shoulders match the down slope so that my left shoulder was also slightly lower than my right. When I matched my shoulders to the hill the club face would have less effective loft and therefore the flight of the ball would be lower. Once again, the ball will tend to do what the hill does, and since this hill sloped downward the ball flight would tend to be lower. To offset this lower ball flight I selected a more lofted wood. I would normally use my 5 wood if the lie were flat, but because the downhill angle was relatively severe I used my 9 wood. When I took my practice swings I made sure that my shoulders matched the hill, knowing that I was doing this correctly when the club head swept grass smoothly

# Hole 7

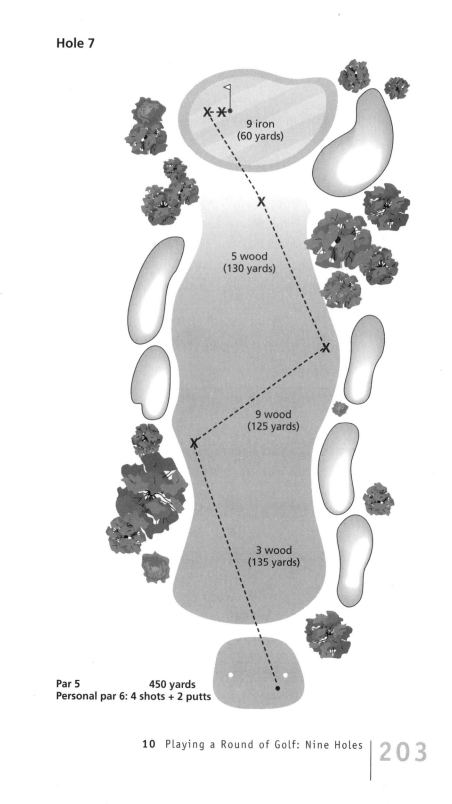

9 iron
(60 yards)

5 wood
(130 yards)

9 wood
(125 yards)

3 wood
(135 yards)

Par 5          450 yards
Personal par 6: 4 shots + 2 putts

down the hill. Because this was a more difficult lie for me I took an extra practice swing to be comfortable with the setup.

*Results:* I hit the 9 wood relatively well, and as planned the ball flight was lower than normal. I aimed into the right side of the fairway to help to avoid the bunker guarding the left side of the approach to the green. My golf ball traveled 125 yards.

**Fairway wood:** I still had a long distance to my green, so it was unnecessary for me to know the actual yardage, as there was no major trouble to avoid. I used my 5 wood and aimed into the right side of the fairway to avoid the fairway bunkers on the left.

*Results:* My 5 wood was straight but very low because I did not hit the ground quite enough. I could see a pattern developing, with my shots traveling lower, so I stepped aside while my other playing partners were hitting and took a few extra practice swings, making sure that the bottom of the club hit the ground. My 5 wood traveled 130 yards into the right side of the fairway.

**Approach shot:** I had 60 yards to the center of the green and the pin was located in the back-left corner. The green was also slightly elevated, so I planned on a 75-yard shot to compensate for the pin being in the back of the green and the green being elevated. When I consulted my yardage chart, I saw that for 75 yards I needed my 9 iron.

*Results:* My 9 iron was straight again, as I am always very careful to aim precisely when approaching the green. Once again I did not hit the ground quite enough and the ball traveled a little bit too low, rolling to the back of the green just past the pin. I had a fifteen-foot downhill putt remaining.

**Fifteen-foot putt:** Because my fifteen-foot putt was downhill, I was especially careful with the speed. I rolled the ball the right distance and respected the difficulty of the slope, gripping lower on the putter to help me to control speed and distance. Because the slope was so severe, I picked my target to be short of the actual cup, pretending this was where I was putting to. After I carefully aimed my face and aligned my body, always reminding myself to keep my lower body still, I repeated what I felt in my practice stroke, with the ball.

*Results:* My ball rolled very nicely to within six inches of the cup—just short. I was very happy with this result, and while it would have been very nice if the ball had rolled a little bit farther, this was my original goal and I was happy with my personal par of 6.

## Hole #8

> Par 3 • 95 yards • Water down the entire left side of the hole • Personal par 3 (1 shot+ 2 putts)

**Tee shot:** The yardage to the center of the green was 95 yards and the wind was slightly in my face, so I thought the hole would play 100 yards in total. My 5 iron travels somewhere between 95 and 105 yards and I am much more comfortable with it than I am with my 4 iron, so this was my club of choice. I placed my tee in the left side of the tee box, because this was the side of the trouble, and I aimed to the right side of the green to avoid the water hazard. Once again I teed my golf ball slightly higher than normal to compensate for the fact that I was having difficulty hitting the ground enough. I also made sure that my practice swing was realistic in tempo and hit the ground. I found this hole particularly difficult to aim because of the hazard on the left, so I was careful to pick an intermediate target to aim my ball over. To accomplish this, after I took my practice swing I stood directly behind my golf ball so that it was between me and my target and picked a spot on the ground to aim over, called an intermediate target. I used this spot to help aim my club face and set my body parallel to the line between my ball and the spot.

*Results:* My 5 iron was very solid but curved to the right, so I ended up pin high just off of the edge of the green. While I would have preferred to be on the putting surface I was somewhat happy with this result and did the best I could to hit my short shot close enough to the pin to one-putt.

**Short-game shot:** I had a good lie, so all options were available to me. I had approximately 3 steps of ground to carry and 15 steps of green to work with. Because I needed more roll than

# Hole 8

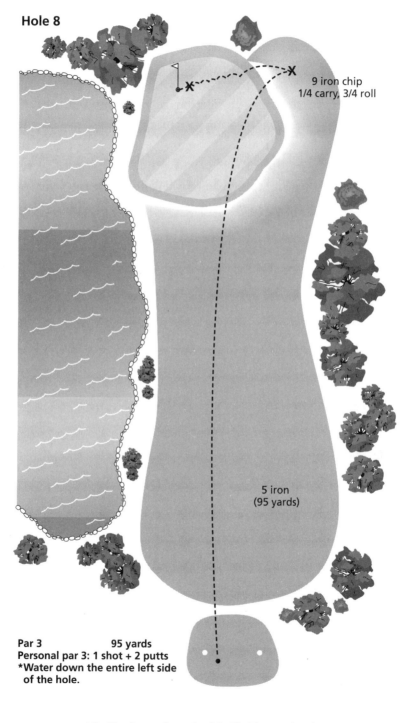

9 iron chip
1/4 carry, 3/4 roll

5 iron
(95 yards)

Par 3          95 yards
Personal par 3: 1 shot + 2 putts
*Water down the entire left side
  of the hole.

carry and was within 5 steps of the green I chipped. Because of the percentage of roll needed I used my 9 iron and attempted to land the ball one-quarter of the way to the pin. When I took my practice strokes I reminded myself to lean to my left and make sure that the bottom of my 9 iron brushed the grass. When I decided how big a stroke to take I was sure to look where I wanted the ball to land when it came out of the air. After aiming my 9 iron face carefully and building my setup around the face, with one more reminder to lean to my left, I repeated what I felt in my practice stroke, with the ball in the way.

*Results:* My 9-iron chip was very good and rolled to within one foot of the cup, where I was able to tap in for a par 3 on the hole, also my personal par.

## Hole #9

Par-4 • 290 yards • Water crossing the fairway just short of the green • Personal par 5 (3 shots + 2 putts)

**Tee shot:** Once again I teed off with my 3 wood because I was very comfortable with it at that point. Because the water hazard crossed the fairway just in front of the green, it was necessary for me to lay up, short of the water on my second shot, so that any extra distance I might possibly gain with my driver would be unnecessary. I placed my tee in to the right side of the tee box and aimed to the left side of the fairway, planning for a slight left-to-right curving of the ball that I saw on my tee shot on the eighth hole.

*Results:* My 3-wood shot went as planned. It traveled 140 yards into the left center of the fairway and it did curve slightly left to right. Because my predominant ball flight is left to right, I played for that tendency on the golf course. At my next lesson I mentioned it to my golf professional because I knew I was sacrificing some potential distance.

**Fairway shot:** I had 80 yards to lay up short of the water hazard that crossed the fairway just in front of the green. I knew that to lay up just short of the green was 70 yards from the center of the green, so to arrive at this distance I subtracted 70 from the 150 yards I had left in total yardage. My best 9 iron travels 80 yards, so this was the club that I used because I wanted to be sure to stay short of the water.

*Results:* My 9 iron was fine but still a little bit too low because I did not quite hit the ground enough. It was time to do some of my scrape drills on the golf course to help me isolate the feeling

Hole 9

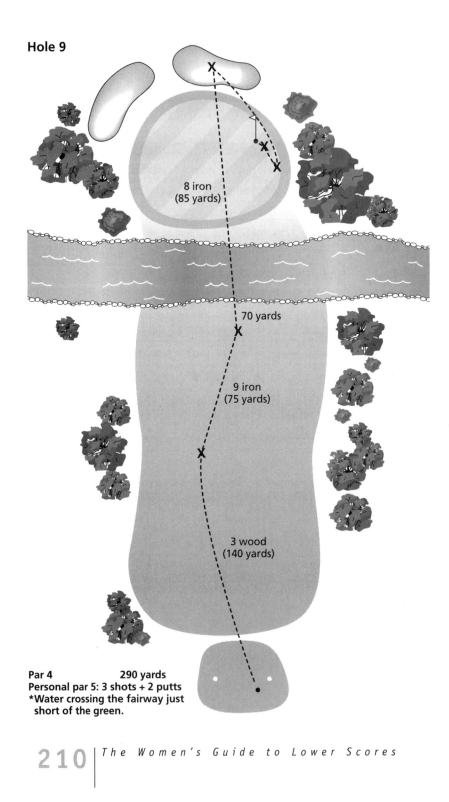

8 iron
(85 yards)

70 yards

9 iron
(75 yards)

3 wood
(140 yards)

Par 4          290 yards
Personal par 5: 3 shots + 2 putts
*Water crossing the fairway just
  short of the green.

when the club stays low enough to the ground to get the ball into the air. My golf ball rolled to just short of the 70-yard mark, leaving 75 yards to the center of the green.

**Approach shot:** I had 75 yards to the center of the green, and because I had to go over the water I reminded myself that it was better to be long than to be short. When I checked my yardage chart I saw that my 8 iron, when I hit it just OK, traveled 75 yards, so this was the club I used. Because it was extremely important that my club hit the ground to get the ball into the air over the water hazard I took one or two extra practice swings, making sure that I heard the club thump the ground. I realized that I was taking a little more time than I prefer. Because the water made me nervous I allowed myself a little longer preparation time.

*Results:* My 8 iron was solid, and for this I was happy, but unfortunately the ball traveled too far and flew over the back of the green into a greenside bunker.

**Greenside bunker:** I reminded myself that to make it easier to take sand I would position my golf ball to the left of the center of my stance, hold my hands very high on the grip of the club, and dig my feet into the sand. All of these setup adjustments help to throw the sand out of the bunker. Once I set up I made just my normal golf swing and attempted to throw the sand out of the bunker and onto the green, paying special attention to go to a full finish where my right foot rotates up to the toe. It was especially important to take sand, because I did not want the ball to travel too far and land in the water hazard. I also was a little more careful to aim slightly left of the flag. In case I did not hit the bunker shot perfectly, my ball would have a greater chance to stop, because there was more distance at that angle back to the hazard.

*Results:* My bunker shot was OK, although the ball traveled a little bit too far back toward the front of the green. I was happy that I aimed left of the flag and away from the water, as this may have saved me at least one shot by keeping my golf ball in play. I had a thirty-foot putt remaining, uphill and slightly right to the left.

**Thirty-foot putt:** I had a longer putt, slightly uphill and right to left, so I aimed slightly to the right and just past the cup to compensate for the curving and the uphill. I took my practice strokes looking at this spot. After carefully aiming my face and aligning my body I attempted to putt the ball to this new imaginary cup.

*Results:* My thirty-foot putt was very solid but came up a little bit short, leaving a four-foot tester to complete my nine holes.

**Four-foot putt:** I really wanted to make this four-foot putt, so I was very careful in aiming at the wording on the ball and my putter face. After I took my practice strokes, looking at the back of the cup because I had a straight, flat putt, I gave myself a little extra insurance and slightly turned in my toes, making sure that my lower body stayed very still.

*Results:* The four-foot putt went into the cup in one more than my personal par. While I would have preferred to have made a 5 on this hole I was pleased to have played smart enough to avoid the water hazard.

## After-Round Assessment

After my golf round I like to go through what happened, so as to help my practice time improve my weaknesses. Based upon these nine holes, I needed to double-check my grip to help to minimize the tendency of the ball curving from left to right. I also checked my posture and distance from the golf ball to help to improve my contact. My practice time involved making myself earn each golf ball by taking a practice swing that hit the ground before I allowed myself to hit a ball.

I was happy with my course management and, other than a few contact errors, I thought I played quite intelligently. While my chips were very solid, I felt that I could work a little more on my distance control by repeating the same chip shot to the same target to help develop my feel for controlling distance. I also slightly struggled with getting some of my longer putts close to the hole, so I did the back-and-forth drill with two cups that are relatively far apart. In this drill I have to two-putt or better five times in a row and do not allow myself to leave until I accomplish this goal. I also gave myself a little more time to roll longer putts before my next round and was sure to discuss all of these concerns with my golf professional in our next lesson, as my quest for lower scores continued.

# Conclusion:
# Its Up to You!

**11**

**S**o here you have it! Here are the necessary tools you need to lower your golf scores, with many options to choose from. By quantifying your skills through testing you can have a better idea what your game plan should include when you are on the golf course. You can also use these results to identify the areas that need special attention when you do practice. By improving your fundamentals and the ability to be aware when your attempts are being made correctly, you can be your own coach and have a more productive practice time.

Your short game is the quickest way to lower your scores, and the short-game cheat sheet allows you to immediately lower your scores by teaching you to ask yourself specific questions that allow you to choose the best short-game shot for each situation. You don't even need to practice to do this—and isn't that good news!

Use your shortcut checks and quick tips to improve each of your short-game areas as well as your full swing.

Once you have a stronger concept and better shot selection, you can add the right attitude and better strategy, which will also help you lower your scores. All these areas are addressed in the sample nine holes, together with the thought process involved in playing a round. You might find this information best applied a little bit at a time, as you will not hear what I am saying or digest what you are reading until you are ready for it. Don't despair; I see this over and over again in my teaching. Whatever area seems to help you the most is where you should start, and then, once you feel you have accomplished that goal, try moving onto the next.

Now, it is all up to you! If you are willing to open your mind and learn new techniques, you can score lower. Have fun!

# Appendix

**H**ere's a copy of a yardage chart that you can fill in, laminate, and attach to your golf bag. The goal here is to make you more self-sufficient, allowing you to make better, more educated decisions on choosing the proper club. You may not have some of the clubs listed on the next page, or you may have one that is not listed, and that is fine. Fill in the clubs that you do have, and if you have one that is not listed, just add that to the bottom. You may want to make an extra copy or two to keep in your golf bag, just in case.

**Yardage Chart**

Sand Wedge:

Gap Wedge:

Pitching Wedge:

9 iron:

8 iron:

7 iron:

6 iron:

5 iron:

4 iron:

11 wood:

9 wood:

7 wood:

5 wood:

3 wood:

1 wood:

## Uneven Lies Cheat Sheet

**Uphill Lie: left foot higher than right**
Match shoulders to the hill
Golf ball will fly higher: use a less lofted club

**Downhill lie: left foot lower than right**
Match shoulders to the hill
Golf ball will fly lower: use a more lofted club

**Sidehill lie: ball above feet**
Grip lower on club
Ball will tend to curve left: aim more right

**Sidehill lie: ball below feet**
Step closer to golf ball
Ball will tend to curve right: aim more left

# Short-Game Cheat Sheet—Simplified

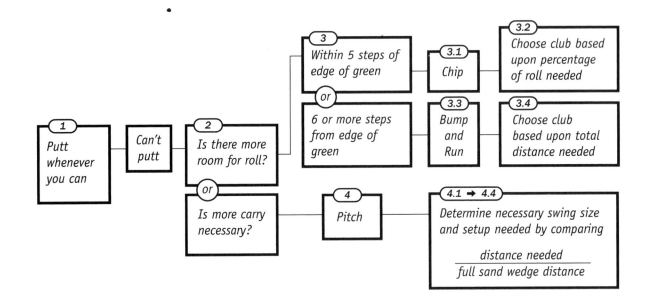